Dedication

Coming out with bold writing on parenting is not so easy, unless the characters involved in the same does not warrant the authenticity of the subject and the author. Since, this is not a fiction work, but purely and totally a practical implementation, the main characters involved, in fact, the sole characters are the children, mother and father. Entire writing revolves around these people. Being a father of a son, author of this novel thought, husband of a woman, son of someone, uncle of nephews and nieces, teacher of many, etc. I credit everything to the foresaid.

Since, this book is totally about shaping kids as desired, I would lovingly and gratefully dedicate all of this to the fourteen years of my amazing journey with my son Joash Marvel, sixteen years of marvelous togetherness with my wife Rebekah Hemanth. I feel very happy and glad that you made almost all my thoughts, experiments, implementations come true. If not you, then either this master art of my pen would remain a mere fiction or I would have abruptly dropped penning this idea.

Not forgetting to mention my God, my Lord, my Savior Jesus Christ, the only worthy above everyone to be honored and dedicated this book.

FOREWORD

I am very glad to have been given the opportunity to write the foreword to this exceptional book on parenting by my dear friend, Hemanth Kumar Makkena. As a parent myself and someone who deeply values the importance of faith, I am elated to see a resource that addresses the crucial role of parents in raising their children with strong family values.

In today's fast-paced and ever-changing world, the task of parenting has become increasingly challenging. As parents, we are faced with numerous hurdles and uncertainties as we strive to impart wisdom, morality, and faith to our children. This book comes as a much-needed guiding light, providing practical insights rooted in real-life experiences and scriptural wisdom.

Hemanth Kumar Makkena has masterfully woven together the timeless teachings of the Bible with relatable examples from everyday life. By doing so, he has made parenting not only accessible but also relevant to the modern world. It is evident that this book is the product of sincere dedication, extensive research, and a profound understanding of the challenges faced by parents today.

33 MARVELOUS MANTRAS
FOR ARTFUL PARENTING

Hemanth Kumar Makkena

Chennai • Bangalore

CLEVER FOX PUBLISHING
Chennai, India

Published by CLEVER FOX PUBLISHING 2023
Copyright © Hemanth Kumar Makkena 2023

All Rights Reserved.
ISBN: 978-93-56484-87-0

This book has been published with all reasonable efforts taken to make the material error-free after the consent of the author. No part of this book shall be used, reproduced in any manner whatsoever without written permission from the author, except in the case of brief quotations embodied in critical articles and reviews.

The Author of this book is solely responsible and liable for its content including but not limited to the views, representations, descriptions, statements, information, opinions and references ["Content"]. The Content of this book shall not constitute or be construed or deemed to reflect the opinion or expression of the Publisher or Editor. Neither the Publisher nor Editor endorse or approve the Content of this book or guarantee the reliability, accuracy or completeness of the Content published herein and do not make any representations or warranties of any kind, express or implied, including but not limited to the implied warranties of merchantability, fitness for a particular purpose. The Publisher and Editor shall not be liable whatsoever for any errors, omissions, whether such errors or omissions result from negligence, accident, or any other cause or claims for loss or damages of any kind, including without limitation, indirect or consequential loss or damage arising out of use, inability to use, or about the reliability, accuracy or sufficiency of the information contained in this book.

One of the aspects that make this book stand out is its focus on the practicality of parenting. Rather than offering abstract theories and detached advice, Hemanth has taken great care to present tangible, actionable guidance that parents can readily apply in their lives. He acknowledges the complexities of parenting and addresses various scenarios that parents often encounter, be it in navigating technology, addressing peer pressure, or dealing with moral dilemmas. This book serves as a trusted companion for parents in their day-to-day journey of nurturing their children.

Throughout the pages of this book, Hemanth emphasizes the significance of grounding parenting practices in the scriptures. By relying on biblical principles, he encourages parents to develop a deeper understanding of their roles and responsibilities. It is this spiritual foundation that empowers parents to raise children who are not only equipped to face the challenges of life but also inspired to walk on the path of righteousness and faith.

I wholeheartedly endorse this book and encourage all parents, regardless of their age and cultural background, to read it attentively. Parenting carries within it the potential to transform lives. As parents, we often find ourselves caught up in the busyness of daily routines, unintentionally neglecting the profound impact we have on our children's lives. Hemanth's book serves as a powerful reminder that time is of the essence and that the formative years of our children's lives demand our focused attention.

To the parents who read this book, I hope it will ignite a newfound motivation within you. Let it inspire you to be intentional in your parenting, to be present for your children, and to instill in them the values that will guide them on their journey of growth and discovery. May you find encouragement and strength through these pages to nurture your children's hearts and souls in the light of God's love.

In conclusion, I express my heartfelt gratitude to Hemanth Kumar Makkena for penning this invaluable Mantras for parents. Let us embrace this opportunity to shape the future generation with faith, love, and unwavering devotion.

Dr. Rajesh, PhD,
Principal,
ACTS Academy of Higher Education, Bangalore

PREFACE

*W*hile taking another bold step after contributing great pearls of wisdom in my previous books (1) **A Lens That Zooms The Happy World,** (2) **Simply Kidding – 33 Wisdom Steps For Ideal Prenting** (3) **Saral Parvarish – Aadarsh Parvarish Ke 33 Buddhimattata Kadam** (4) **Mastering Myself – A Secret To Subdue Hell Bent Powers,**' the reader, you still continue to be the major portion of my thoughts and ideas. The insights, wisdom and revelations of '**33 Marvelous Mantras For Artful Parenting**' comes majorly from many people who came across in my life with variety of struggles, challenges and sufferings.

And hence, first and foremost, I hereby dedicate to you, the reader, the entire success of my previous writings as well as the reason for the present one. Not limiting myself and sound stingy in expressing my heart behind this writing, it would be right for me to pour it out and say that this is not an ordinary book which just evolved or popped out from nowhere or out of some imaginations, inspirations and external motivations. This is purely a careful experimental, observational, and a daring implementation of the revelations and wisdom that got conceived in my thoughts as an answer for all your worries and cares. As you proceed to read this piece of wise literature, it is advised that you don't just read it like a story book, but take time to use it as a handbook. Right way of applying this counsel will yield desired results in shaping lives.

I have been spending my whole lifetime in creating a world in me and for myself. It's been more than four decades now, and the time has arrived to declare that my virtual world has come into reality. So, not wanting to bind and limit those great pearls of wisdom and experimental results to remain just with me and also perish after me, I have penned down step by step parenting, a parenting manual to that part of the world which is also dreaming for a Happy, Joyful, Fruitful, And Prosperous family.

Having a childhood divided, with parents for some period, away from them in hostel, some part with extended family, and back at home during teens, and later almost having a self-dependent period for more than a decade, pained with the sting of financial insufficiency, unmet desires and so on have left me with many questions, longing and craving for more love, affection, attachment etc. Therefore, I decided to find/discover the unfound/undiscovered and gift them to the world that needs the most.

Living with hurt upon losing two of my offspring for medical reasons, which also hit my wife very badly, but thankfully and gratefully to God being kind unto her and strengthening her with extended life on the earth, I am here directing the pointer at you, requiring your attention to focus on the ray of hope, and way of life that is very well at your hand, if you just care and look for it.

Since, the initial part on the subject parenting in my previous book 'Simply Kidding – 33 Wisdom Steps For Ideal Parenting' revolves around preconception, conception, fetus, and ends with toddler age, my personal experiences and learnings begin with our premature still born first baby girl, whom we chose to call Shekinah Marvel, our third baby boy Loretto Sam, also a premature born, who suffered multiple ailments and spent all his days in treating himself on the ventilator, without seeing his earthly home left this world after facing the killer battle for ten days. The continuation of the same subject moving to toddler ages gets extended with our second child Joash Marvel, a fourteen-year-old boy, enormous contributor of my learnings and experiences in parenthood along with my wife Rebekah.

Being in the field of care and counselling for nearly two decades, listening and addressing to the challenges faced by the parents in upbringing, their infants, adolescents, teens and youth, I felt the need to come out with this volume as a guide, handy tool and preventive measure **'Simply Kidding – 33 Wisdom Steps For Ideal Parenting'** for the newly wedded, yet to be parents, guiding and corrective measures to the parents of adolescents' and teens through **'33 Marvelous Mantras For Artful Parenting'**. These books also serve as a remedy in undoing most of the wrong parentings to a greater extent. They focus on the parenting challenges and their kid's responses and reactions. As an additional top up for all your actions and reactions, emotions management, (anger, hatred, jealousy, selfishness, rebellion, bullied, depression, failures, rejection, abandonment, etc. find out my another master piece **Mastering Myself – A Secret To Subdue Hell Bent Powers.** Do look for all my writings at online stores.

ACKNOWLEDGEMENT

The following words comes straight from my heart that weighs more than any other precious value of the world. There are few people involved in bringing out this volume of practical wisdom into print form, and they need to be very specially acknowledged and thanked. Since, I am not just an observer, thinktank, researcher, learner, but also an orator and teacher of my findings, my daily/regular readers on WhatsApp, Facebook and audience in person, at various platforms, beneficiaries of individual and family counselling are the contributors of several ideas and reason to discover solutions for their struggles and challenges through **'33 Marvelous Mantras For Artful Parenting.'**

My son Joash Marvel Makkena and my wife Rebekah Makkena, you have been my proud instruments in my life management laboratory that gave away the exact results of my experimentation with family and parenting. Without you this creative design of a happy, stress-free, struggleless, smooth and blessed form of living is impossible. Your actions and reactions are the real peace and joy of my heart. They are the priceless jewels in my unfading crown of wisdom literature.

Acknowledgement

The most special person who need to be acknowledged here is Eben Paturi, a sixteen-year-old boy, who also subjected himself to my upbringing. Today I am proud and bold to mention his name acknowledging, because he has come out with fair and clean natured personality. I am indebted to his mother Elizabeth Paturi, my wife's sister and her husband Barnabas Paturi who blindly and silently allowed him in my care. Even in times of harsh measures, they are still very cooperative, understanding and helpful to have my inputs work, other than what I get from my son and my wife.

My congregational infants, adolescents, teens and youth, plenty in number who call me Pappa, and are submissive to my care, concern, corrections, etc. are the very important people here to be mentioned, and I say a very big thank you and lots of love to you all. Their parents stand at a very honorable position for their respect and faith on me, allowing their wards to be brought up in my discipline. I am immensely happy to see all of you coming out with bright colors.

Special thanks to my first audience, approver and proof reader of my works, my wife Rebekah Hemanth and a helping hand with creative designs and ideas, my son Joash Marvel. My parents, my in-laws and all my well-wishers and supporters.

Many newly wedded couples, young mothers and fathers regularly sent me feedbacks as they are my first readers and audience on several above-mentioned platforms. Wishing that the world near and far would richly benefit with this novel, unique masterpiece from my pen. Thus, here I announce that, **'33 Marvelous Mantras For Artful Parenting'** after 'Simply Kidding - 33 Wisdom Steps

Acknowledgement

For Ideal Parenting' is another gift unto you from someone who really cares!

I do allocate little space but in great words to the publisher of this book, Clever Fox Publishing and the entire team for their dedicated, committed, prompt, efficient and creative services in printing, designing, publishing and assurances of post publication services along with distribution, marketing and promotional activities globally.

TABLE OF CONTENTS

Mantra 1. A Beast, A Demon, A Saint Or An Angel 1

Mantra 2. Cord-less Cat 6

Mantra 3. Returning Tomorrow - Invested Today 11

Mantra 4. All For Tomorrow 16

Mantra 5. The beginning of the new experience 21

Mantra 6. Clearing The Ground For The Next 26

Mantra 7. Preventive Headaches 32

Mantra 8. Junking Distance 37

Mantra 9. Expensive Artists 42

Mantra 10. Greed And Theft 47

Mantra 11. Wait For No One 53

Mantra 12. The Source That Springs 60

Mantra 13. Outsmarting the Smart 65

Mantra 14. Respectful Lens 70

Mantra 15. More Ghastly Than Civil And World Wars 75

Mantra 16. A Stick And A Minute Clock 80

Mantra 17. Trouble Shooting 85

Table Of Contents

Mantra 18. They Won't Come Back Again 91

Mantra 19. Empty Bags 97

Mantra 20. Holistic I Love You 103

Mantra 21. Time For Saying I Love You 110

Mantra 22. Correcting The Memories 116

Mantra 23. Orbital Order 121

Mantra 24. Many Moods But One Mode 127

Mantra 25. Culprit Home 133

Mantra 26. Home Theatre 139

Mantra 27. No Mood Day 144

Mantra 28. End of preaching And Punishing 149

Mantra 29. Make Ambitious 154

Mantra 30. Stop Comparing And Taunting 159

Mantra 31. Complaining Moms And Bashing Dads 164

Mantra 32. Are You Satisfied 169

Mantra 33. Make Your Own 174

Mantra 1

A BEAST, A DEMON, A SAINT OR AN ANGEL

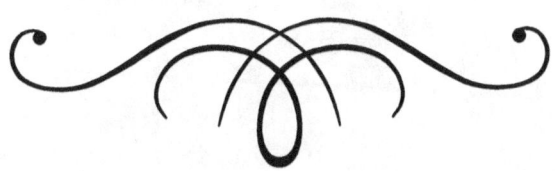

Winds and storms have their purposes. They possess exceedingly great and strong powers with destructive forces. They are never the same in nature every time, but occasional and situational. They are inseparable part of the nature and universe. They are soft, loving and life giving, as long as they remain mere breeze and rain. They become fatal and threatening, once their speed and force of movement picks up the pace and keep whirling until their all power and strength comes to almost nothing. But before that, they uproot so much of the part of the earth, be that plantation, constructed structures, living beings etc.

All that exist on the land, of the air, and of the water have natural powers, they are either to sustain themselves from those natural destructive forces or are the ways and plans to escape them. Those, who or which are weak to withstand such powers, have no strong base, have no ideas and plans to keep themselves safe, either by preventive or defending methods. Such people turn out to be the victims and the losers. Any structure, invention or creation before being brought into existence is equipped with safety measures to withstand any kind of natural and unnatural threats and dangers. In the absence of or because of the powerlessness of the safety standards, many things and people will get shifted to unknown and strange destinations with injuries, hurts, breakages, damages and irreparable loss.

Stronger things/beings have strong life; weaker things/beings have weak life. Powerful and planned things/beings have longer life; fragile and unplanned things/beings have shorter life. The powers, forces, pace, situations and circumstances of life never were, are and will be kind unto the weaker sections. They appear ghastly and merciless before the unplanned, ignorant, careless and reckless ones. They become weak, powerless and dead before the vigilant, wise, alert, cautious, unwavering and firm.

Having a family, especially the inclusion of a spouse, child or children, relatives and extended families comes with additional pleasant/unpleasant powers, forces, emotions, actions, reactions, situations, circumstances, etc. Since, every individual is a different person, the addition of one after the other in the family or life is the addition and involvement of their powers, forces, thoughts, feelings, reactions, ideologies, beliefs etc. The more the people are added or attached, the individual's day to day dealings with them increases. Handling them tactfully and wisely require maturity, presence of mind, timely actions, and most importantly, willingness to deal without damage and loss.

The arrival of new born at the very first moment brings unmeasured joy and happiness. Parents and all those around the infants get filled with the fulness of love and affection. The innocent and tiny little beings arrive with mighty power of attraction and bonding. They possess happy energy that can fill every heart and make them create a beautiful smile on their faces. But with the growth of those babies each passing day, the decline in their loving, happy, attracting and bonding energies are usually witnessed. Gradually, they begin to acquire negative energies in them, they become fussy, impatient, disobedient, rebellious, quarrelsome, abusive etc. This is where the actual parenting turns into challenging mode.

The change in the human beings is very natural and must take place, otherwise it can be seen as the absence of mind and senses. Every single thought produced inside, every single thing that is seen, heard and sensed makes the brain and the heart to work. They make humans either to accept what was sent inside or to reject them. The conclusion of that work turns out to be the behavior of the individuals. They in turn again produce different kind of energies that can be either good or bad. The pleasant breeze that arrived with new born life and the blessed atmosphere all around could now become unpleasant winds and storms that can whirl our entire lives, tossing up and up and throw away at broken and damaged destinations.

For every action another reaction is produced. If the reactions are simple, calm, understanding, mature and wise, then the atmosphere around us can never be changed by any kind of behavior that knocks on our hearts to disrupt the beautiful pleasant weather we created for ourselves. But if those reactions are hard, rough, angered, swift and powerful, then the entire weather could immediately become hot and mad. As the first lesson concludes with introductory lines, you are asked to think, what our kids are trying to take out of us or make us, 'a saint, an angel, a beast or demon?' They have the power to make us anything, if we are not careful and watchful in our parenting.

Mantra 2

CORD-LESS CAT

*I*t is always very easy to imitate, but it might be difficult to follow. Reproducing the invented or discovered could be an effort filled practice, but it is tough and many a times impossible to find or create something new. It doesn't take any special talent or wisdom to watch, it doesn't require academic qualifications to observe, it doesn't demand great and genius minds to learn; all it requires is a brake to stop and think for alternative. A question to ask yourself, 'what if, I listen to my own mind and follow my own heart?' It even requires a direction to steer your life from age-old practices to need based applications; and the rest will be your guidelines for coming ages.

A priestly family from the Cat lovers land of India, Kolkata, has a practice of tying a cat with a cord or belt and locked to the window bars. This custom had been in practice for many generations. Thankfully, the great grandmother was alive and active to teach, and also to answer to the questions of the fourth-generation great granddaughter. Once, on a very common day of the ritual, the little girl asked her mother before tying the cat to the window bars, why is this pet needed here during this practice? Her mother, who doesn't know the reason simply directed unto her mother, saying, 'I don't know. My mother used to do it; I am just following her. Better you ask my mom.'

The little girl got the same response from her grandmother. Finally, the great grandmother with a silly smile on her face replied, 'my cat used to disturb me while I was on my religious practices, so I used to tie her to the window and perform my acts without any disturbance. My daughter watched me do that and she imitated this method. Her daughter found this as a custom and decided to pass it on to your generation. I am glad you questioned me about this and I hope that you will let your cat free!'

The fourth-generation child, who found that her mother and grandmother simply watched, observed, imitated and followed, but did not think what they were doing, had an alternative to change the direction. She untied her Cat from being a part of that practice. She already taught her pet to listen to her and follow the instructions. Now, all the four generations are enjoying their doings along with the pet, since, it doesn't disturb them anymore but gets involved in the act and enjoys along with them. All the prior three generations now understood that, knowing, understanding, teaching even the pets to adopt our discipline is neither difficult, nor impossible.

Having kids, having them around us, not that big nor that mature to adopt our system of living, neither willing nor obedient, uncontrollable and stubborn, disturbing and attention seekers, and we have serious businesses to carry forward; what best traditional ways of dealing with them do we have other than warning, shouting, scolding, slapping, beating, kicking or bribing with desired things or tying to electronically internet cords etc.? They suit best and everyone applies one or more of them for every situation and finds momentary relief.

Not every child has same mood and tuning, neither every family or parent possess the same; some are fussy and stubborn; weak at body and mind; angry and rude in nature; ill-mannered and ill tempered in behavior; lazy, untidy, unhygienic in personal attention; sharp, smart, studios, genius but disobedient, irresponsible, careless, in household matters etc. Every child is a challenge and every kind of parenting is challenging too. What we find here unique and simple is, nothing is too difficult nor is impossible. Every nut-bolt and screw have their perfectly fitting spanners and drivers not just to tighten them but also to loosen for desired alignment. So is Artful Parenting, it throws light on every area of challenge and challenging parenting. Before we reach to the next Mantra, make sure you have your cat freed, staying around but having learnt your system.

Mantra 3

RETURNING TOMORROW - INVESTED TODAY

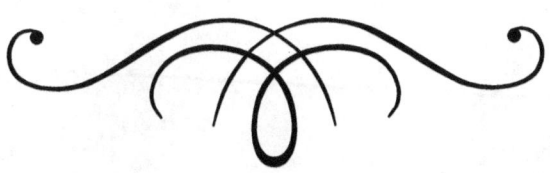

*H*aving gone through the alternative way for inventive and creative parenting, a need-based methodology, the informatory warning makes its place here before allowing the author to proceed with our topic and subject. And that caution comes with few questions, rather than a statement. What's wrong with the traditional way of parenting, which has seen hundreds of generations and few millenniums? Was every parenting method of the past wrong? Wasn't that meeting the needs? Hasn't that seen thousands and millions groomed well? Weren't the kids of those ages including us, a product, refined and greatly successful? Aren't the societies, states, nations and the worlds seeing the desired and expected results?

Absolutely, there's no denial that few millenniums and hundreds of generations had passed through billions of parenting phases, each one in its own way, but majorly through the traditional ones that has so much of anger, punishment, abuse, neglect, reject, hatred, abandonment, harsh and rude behavior involved. The answer to the above questions comes in the question form itself, isn't every child rightful to live a life with respect, dignity; free from all kinds of harsh and rude treatments; free from child labor or financial burdens of the family; being loved, cared, wanted, desired provided every good thing with abundance; with all the necessities supplied; getting the love and care of both the parents; having a life supportive for right upbringing?

If the answers for all these questions are singular and bold 'yes,' then the answers for all the former questions can boldly be singularly yes, with few exceptions here and there. The idea and intent of the author is to enlighten everyone to create a world of their own, which has so much of love, care, concern, harmony, respect, honor, dignity; knowledge, wisdom and understanding towards every area that has making, rectifying and remaking. The author is also desiring to teach the ways and means to have all things met with abundance; and have the reader ultimately build a heaven with heavenly things involved in it.

There's so much of pain, sorrow, grief, agony, hurt, suffering, trouble, trauma, hopelessness in the individuals, which majorly had been birthed in them at the very tender age, right then when they were budding in their infancy and adolescence. Some succeeded to ignore them and moved forward; some to face them with boldness by taking corrective measures; some took them as a challenge to defeat them forever, but others feared living with them, facing them, overcoming them. As a result, the world has people with hurting and harming behaviors. The weak, the scared, the much suffered opts for ending the life through suicide as the one and easy solution. This had been greatly seen in the younger generations that could not withstand the pressures, neglect and rejection.

What we give today will be returned to us tomorrow. When we give the neglected and painful upbringing, we might get abandonment as a return of the future. If abandonment and neglect is one of the reasons for having orphanages, then old age homes also could be the resultant of yesterday's investments. The reason for the existence of these two care centers could be any but should not be neglect and abandonment. Even if all could stay together under one roof as a family, united, but the bitterness, quarrels, fights, disrespect etc. is the continuous and ongoing battle always. The lack of respect towards elders, absence of love and unity among the siblings, care and concern towards the kids is the result of poor parenting and improper upbringing. The divided and mean parenting will result in discord and harvesting hatred.

Everyone looks for his/her own happiness. They don't bother to understand the inner feelings of others. They lack to create a happy world around them. We, through the Artful Parenting will make attempts to discover, invent and create our own happy world, primarily with the very few ones we own, our one or two or three and more kids. Let us begin to treat them rightful heir of all the blessed things we possess and wish to possess. Our endeavor to the creation and recreation of our little world will enlighten many lamps very soon. Let the Mantra to invest good begin today and bring the best returns tomorrow.

Mantra 4

ALL FOR TOMORROW

*H*ave you noticed that you have become the owner or producer of a human life by birthing a child? If yes, then has that been the reason you claim the belongingness of your child? You tag your spouse, child, with a possessive pronoun, 'my'? You demonstrate the possessiveness all the time and also exercise authority. You wish and make sure that all that your kid possesses must be your attributes, your way of thinking and behavior. It is understood and valid that, since you are the owner of your child, only you have every right and authority, either to teach, correct, unteach, discipline in your own way of understanding, to punish or to deal lovingly and tactfully.

Every tree bears the fruit of its own kind. Every parent bear and raises his/her child in his/her own likeness. If you think you are a good tree, then you are absolutely right, your fruit will be the best. If you are contrary to the foresaid, you will give our society the fruits that are harmful and poisonous. The world is formed with the fruitful contribution of every couple. Today, the earth is proudly counting such fruits in billions. At the same time, the societies and the worlds are divided due to the differences in the nature of the fruit. Not every fruit or individual is sweet and pleasant.

Having said that, let the author quote King Solomon of 9th century before Christ's era, who was the wisest of all the people then and even now. He was addressing both the parents and the young ones. He was also a very great teacher, who in his Proverbs, held the position of a teacher, a counselor and also a great parent. His every word and piece of advice makes complete sense. The sincere follower of his sayings can never miss the mark. Firstly, we will see his advice to the young parents, 'train up a child in the way he should go, and when he is old, he will not depart from it.' From the Holy Bible, Proverbs Chapter 22 verse 6.

He doesn't mean about the area of academics, extracurricular activities, but very particularly of character building. Academics are very well taught in the literary centers, but the character of good morals, clean habits, righteous and holy living belong to the training part of the parents, especially the young adults when their child is in tender ages itself. Solomon says, 'if you train the child, showing him/her the future way to go, surely, he/she will never depart from the same.' His focus was also on the spiritual path, which brings down the heavenly, pure and holy wisdom and knowledge that can transform the kids into divine character.

Secondly, advising the young ones, he says, 'if you cease listening to the instruction, you will stray.' Proverbs 19:27. The moment one begins to cease to listen to instruction, advice, correction, the same moment one will stray away from the path of right living. Being a parent, you are making efforts to bring up your child in the way he/she must go, at the same time the child is also taking steps, listening to the instruction and following. We are not dealing particularly with the academics here in our learnings, but of good and clean conduct that will create your heaven and give you a heavenly life. No doubt, we will be touching the matters so as to advise you in the areas of poor performances in the curricular spheres. If the child doesn't perform well in the studies, then it is the most troubling headache for parents. If the child is unruly, ill mannered, quarrelsome, fighter, misbehaving, and being the reason for parents to be summoned before the school authorities, then that is another shameful and hurting part of life.

Peace of mind, dignified and respectful life, free from insulting situations, self-dependent and responsible children with bright colors, is what every parent expects from their kids. If you succeed to achieve this, then major difficulties of your life have been kept away from knocking you down. One must master every art, so must be parenting. The author, as a wise teacher will be taking you through systematic procedures and simplistic steps to master the art of parenting. As you reach the end of this book Artful Parenting, the author is very confident that you will be equipped with every tool and technique to deal any kind of challenging parenting. Let's do it with full dedication and commitment, and work on the Mantra 'all for the sake of a great and happy tomorrow.'

Mantra 5

THE BEGINNING OF THE NEW EXPERIENCE

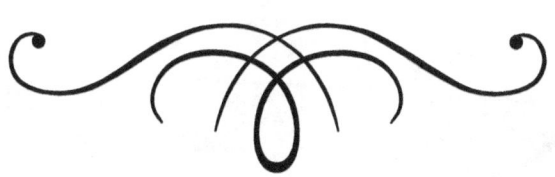

*I*n the concluding chapter of the part one of our Book, Simply Kidding - 33 Wisdom Steps For Ideal Patenting, we dropped the child at the school. Part-One began with choosing ideal and suitable partner and continued parenting lessons with preconception, conception and delivery, reaching to schooling at the end. Here, we continue to take the same forward but, in a dialogue, and dramatic way. We will name the couple that dropped their child at school and are going to pick up now as Raja and Rani. The first born, who is going to be out from first day of the school in a couple of minutes as Raj Kumar. The couple is expecting another member in the family soon and they are preparing ways to welcome new member among them in a very special manner.

Raja and Rani are at the school gate, impatiently waiting to kill the troubling moments of being separated from their pampered one. So are the rest of the parents. Though they express a smile to one another, but in heart are away from present moment. All their thoughts and vision are fixed at the exit gate. Some parents seem to be okay and emotionless; they are the ones who had been completely through this experience and are waiting for their second and some for their third child. The ones who had come to the start of the new experience have lots of anxiety, impatience and nervousness in them.

At last, the wait is over. The school bell rang signaling, it's time to go home. All the toddlers began their tiny steps marching down the lane, searching for their parents in the crowd. Everyone is calling their baby's names. The confused little ones are staring here and there. One after the other each parent reached to their child, with lots of happiness and joy and with lots of love and kisses. Raja and Rani reached their Raj Kumar and did the same as every parent does. They got hold of the child on either sides and began to walk home. Raja made it a point to ask the child of what all happened at the school.

He continued this practice throughout as soon as he gets the child at the school gate. The first thing he used to ask is, how was your day at school? The second thing, what did you learn today as class work? Third, is there any homework? Fourth, any notice from the school? Fifth, any exams coming? Sixth, how were you in the class, any remarks or punishment? He makes honesty the most important element in terms reporting about the study and conduct in class. He does the same thing with his wife Rani too.

He enquires her about her day at office, the experience, dealings with boss, colleagues and subordinates; any difficulties, stress, situation or people trouble her? He always comforts her saying, do not stress yourself to make money. 'You can sit at home and look after the family if you wish to. But I want you to work so that you should not sit idle and simply stare at the television, mobile, computer or through the balcony windows. I don't want you to waste time, life, your learnings, your capabilities, your zeal and enthusiasm. I wish that you shall put them into practice and at work. I also wish that you should work and face the life, present and future, so that you don't need to begin from the scratch if anything happens to me or in case, any calamity hits us hard.'

Raja makes it a point to drop the toddler at school and pick up back. He also drops his wife for work at railway station and picks her back on return. He does this to strengthen the love and the bonding factor. Since, Raja is fortunate to work from home from the very first day of his job, he makes sure to look after the family as well. He gave his spouse so much of relief from many daily chores. He cooks for all three of them, he sends them with their food of the day. After the whole family is reunited in the evening, they enter into the kitchen for preparing dinner. All of them get involved in sharing their daily experiences. After that, they would sit for evening prayers and then for dinner. This is the only meal of the day they would be sharing together, because of being in different locations on different purposes. So, they would never miss this opportunity for any cause. They do this for the reason, when they spend more time together, they will understand each other well and bond together firmly.

Raja used to sing scriptures in the form of song and tell the bed time stories. He also used to share his struggles, experiences both good and bad which can keep his Raj Kumar away from taking any wrong path in the future. He firmly believes in King Solomon's advice, 'train up the child in the way he should go... ' another command from the Holy Bible, Deuteronomy Chapter 6 verse 7, 'You shall teach them diligently to your sons and shall talk of them when you sit in your house and when you walk by the way and when you lie down and when you rise up.' By doing so, every day will begin well and will also end well. The practice that Raja had adopted will keep away all the unwanted away from entering one's life and family too. 'All that begins well will end well,' should be your mantra of life.

Mantra 6

CLEARING THE GROUND FOR THE NEXT

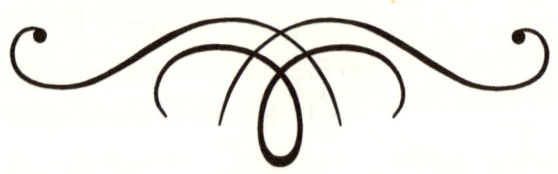

Raja, Rani and Raj Kumar had been living happily with meager income and facilities too. They have adopted adjustable mentality. Raja, while looking for his would-be wife sought similar mindset in his future partner. He specifically asked her to be honest and open about this. He said, 'I don't mind for any other qualities in you, whether they suit me or not, it is immaterial and secondary for me. But the primary and most concerned one which can link you and me to be united and with a strong bond is agreeing mentality, understanding nature, adjustable mindset, cooperative in all my efforts for a happy family and earning ways; supportive in times of trouble, scarcity and at any untoward and unexpected hard hits of life. Matching colors, foods, interests, hobbies, recreations travel etc. can be matched any time later in the future. What matters here the most is, a good match in mind, heart, discipline and conduct.'

He kept all these before her, when he first visited her with his parents and family. Rani too expressed her views, but before that she agreed to all his requirements, saying, 'I have all that you are looking for. And I assure you that you won't find any complaint in this regard. I am a woman, who wishes to build my home, a sweet one. I am looking for a person who can care and love me beyond his capacities. I have no interest in the social status, I am not into glamouring myself beyond the need. I'm not a spendthrift, but I hold the right for all the basic necessities. I am willing to leave my home, my parents, my comforts, all my attachments and feelings of the two decades behind at my home, only by trusting my future partner and deciding to step in his life, home and family.' Raja Was surprisingly staring onto her face for the bullets like points she kept on sending towards him.

She continued, 'If you cry, I will cry with you, if you struggle, I will struggle with you, if you starve, I will starve with you. But, will you see that you won't let me down anywhere, anytime? You can expect anything from me as long as you keep me human and lively. Once you find a dead heart in your partner, that day all your and her dreams and desires will come to an end. If you are willing to be my strong rock, a pillar to lean on, a shoulder for support and most importantly, a trustworthy and genuine, then you can find yes for all your requirements, make me yours and take to your home.' Raja was impressed and found that other than her no other could make right match to be his Rani.

That's how Raja and Rani entered into the wedlock and also were blessed with their school going Raj Kumar. As mentioned in the previous mantra, they have almost come to the welcoming days for their new member, another child in the family. But that doesn't look so easy, since there is a big challenge with Raj Kumar, because he hasn't yet made his mind to welcome another person into his parent's laps. Both Raja and Rani are making their best efforts to teach the infant about caring, sharing and accommodating nature. For which, they had to spend lots of time in clearing the ground. Both the parents had to make several adjustments and sacrifices too. In their every talk and move, they would somehow connect the matter to teach him and convince to accept his next sibling as a caring, protective and provider big brother.

Raja told his son that mom would be going to hospital now to get his sibling. 'Who do you want, a brother or a sister?' Raj Kumar said, he needs a brother to play with him. Raja told him, 'if there are no boys but only girls in the hospital, what will you do? We have actually made a request for a boy, but what if, we won't get the same?' I will adjust, was the little one's answer. 'Okay then, the first thing we have to do is, vacate the bed and keep it prepared for mummy and for the new born baby. Okay?' 'Yes.' nodded the son. 'Then come down and lay here with me on the mat and mattress.' The little one happily jumped down and lay there with his dad, listening to his bedtime favorites and slowly slipped into sleep.

The next morning, Rani is shifted to hospital for delivery. Raja reached there right at the time of delivery. She delivered a healthy baby girl. Both the parents were so happy and the entire family too as well. Rani would be reaching home after three days. Raja now has to prepare the ground for full welcome. He went home and told his Raj Kumar that, 'due to some reasons, we are not able to get you a brother. We got a sister for you. I told the hospital authorities to make sure we get a boy next time. So, they promised me a boy for next. What shall we do now? Shall we prepare our welcome arrangements?'

'Okay! Adjust. Let's prepare' was the lad's response. 'Alright, come on, let's clean the house. Please help me in putting all your toys, books, clothes bags in order. By the time I will finish sweeping and mopping. Here we go.' All cleaned. 'Let's go to the kitchen now and cook something for you, mom and me.' They had been through the entire house setting and even cooking. Raja told his son, 'as soon as the bell rings, I will open the door. You hide behind it. When mummy asks about you, I will say you have gone out to play. After mummy enters inside the bedroom with the baby, I will signal you to come behind me and surprise both of them and welcome them with flowers that you got.'

Rani came in along with the new born baby girl, Raja and his Raj Kumar welcomed both of them as planned. The rest of the parents and family members just waited out and cooperated as per Raja's request for special welcome by his son and him. The flow of dear ones continued for days and all came to still for normal, regular routine. Earlier, there were three in that world, now it has become a world of four. The new arrival is named Raj Kumari. Raj Kumar got glued well with his younger sister and is proved to be really caring, loving, sharing and also sacrificing. He had sacrificed many of his joys for the sake of his younger one. All the efforts and pre-planned tactics did work well and brought smiles and happiness in everyone. For smooth functioning of a hassle-free living, 'clearing the ground' is the only mantra.

Mantra 7

PREVENTIVE HEADACHES

Madness in few cases is an inheritance from parents, but mostly a gift from children. Your children can bring out the nut out of you and may leave you loosened all through your life, if only, you are careless to monitor yourself. And the madness that is inherited from the children can keep on proving you crack in every case and deal. Little negligence may result in total behavioral change. Your soft natured character might become a hardcore discipliner and punisher. Your gentleness can pave way for cruelty and no mercy. Your love in no time can vanish to give birth to a heartless taskmaster. You will be totally changed into a sick, troubled, disturbed and clueless natured very soon. All these can be prevented before they hit you on your head, only, if you can care and learn what all are the causes that might stop you from turning nut.

Raja and his wife had almost mastered this art and are at present having great deal of peace with their Raj Kumar and the little daughter too. They take turns to look after all the household works and also looking after their both kids. They had shared the responsibilities between themselves wisely. Since, Raj Kumari needs mother most, Raja took the charge of Raj Kumar and is helping him mature before age. He had almost succeeded to make his son independent, be it his personal grooming, setting up his bag, packing lunch box, filling water bottle, wearing clothes and shoes etc.

Raj Kumar was told to answer to the alarm set for his school and rise up from the bed without snoozing it. He is prompt and very swift to throw his legs out of the bed. He attends the morning's nature call and brushes his teeth. Meanwhile, Raja would prepare his son's early morning drink, breakfast and also his lunch. Soon after he's finished with brushing his teeth, Raja would give him a nice warm shower. Raj Kumar looks after the next course of actions and stands fully prepared at the door, all set to go to school. Raja would bless him with prayers and drop him at his learning center.

By the time Rani would be out of bed, Raja would prepare the meals for the rest of them. Her maternity leaves are coming to an end. Soon, she will be resuming the office. But till then, there is plenty of time for them to spend quality time with their little princess. Raja is back on his feet again to pick up his son from school. As soon as they reach home, they say prayers, thanking God for uniting them safe after day break.

The rule is set for Raj Kumar to let his father and later to his mother known of what all happened in the day at school. After that, he had to keep the day's class work open, each subject book and place them on the table in front of his father, including the school calendar. He refreshes himself and sits voluntarily for doing his homework. Off late, he adopted some changes by himself, and instead of refreshing, he finishes all his homework first. He feels that might take away procrastination through laziness or playful mood. He then immediately rushes out to play with local friends.

The punctuality and swiftness to wake up, killing that laziness without snoozing the alarm, independently getting ready, grooming himself, doing homework etc. are the reasons that had prevented many headaches and kept both the parents, burden free. Small, little things, if taught at tender ages, will become a part of life as inseparables. That is what called the personal discipline. Majority of the parents think, it is heavy burden on the little ones. But Raja believes that it is the right age and right way of parenting. Since, this not only makes your child responsible and self-disciplined but also will give you good health and peace of life.

Those who think about it otherwise and neglected to follow this methodology, have ended up in troublesome living and messy parenting. It saddens, when parents literally struggle hard only to bring their children out of bed from sleep itself. The courses of action after that are no lesser than working in a circus for them. By the time their children get ready and leaves for school, their blood pressure levels would have changed several times for several levels. Checking their classwork and making them to do their homework and to make them sit for studies is yet another cinema altogether. Isn't it wise then by disciplining your ward at right age with right parenting and learn the mantra to prevent many a headaches that might spin you round and round?

Mantra 8

JUNKING DISTANCE

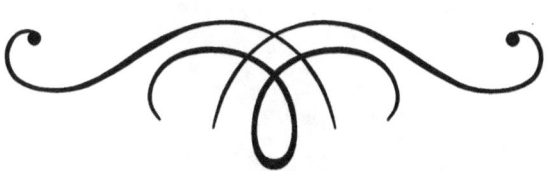

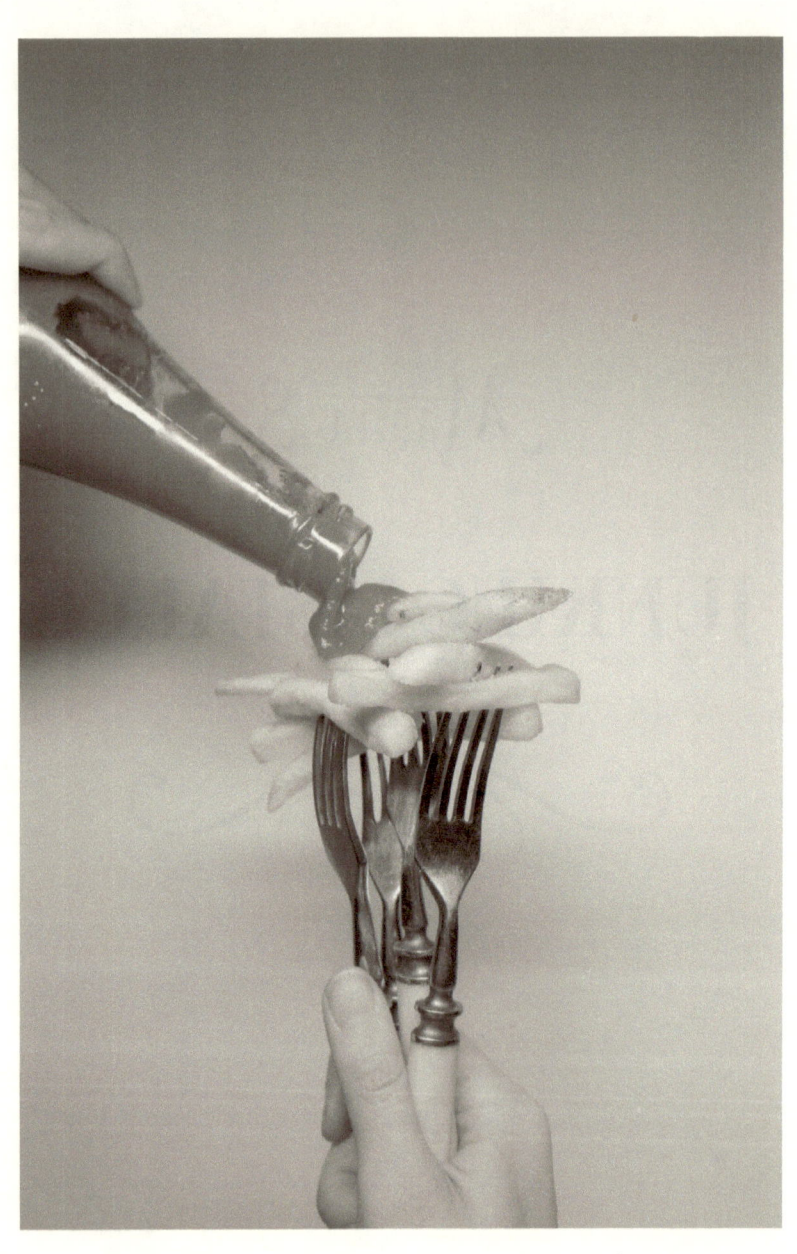

The impression, 'building a golden palace is easier than raising a child,' seldom leaves a permanent mark on human minds with giving up mindset, before the course of parenting begins. Bringing up a child, healthy, clean, disciplined, efficient, active, studios, sharp, smart, obedient, loving, respectful one, is often seen as practically impossible dream. But still, the dream somewhere in the corner of the mind exists, whether hopeful or bleak. Almost all the humans miss out some or many fundamentals at the right age. We travel a far distance and look back for some help, assistance or learning, and that returns only in the form of fundamentals. Fundamental learning, fundamental implications yield appropriate and the desired. Failing which, travelling in reverse becomes the only way. For a fundamentally perfect, there never arises the need to travel back, nor to look for outward help.

The child gets every taste and experience from home and parents. All that available at home, be it good or bad, food or drink, custom or culture, literacy or illiteracy etc. The child can only adopt other than these, only upon exposure to the same in the later days. Coming to the point of child's eating habits, and choice of foods, all that the parents bring in and gets the child to exposed are the only ones that he/she may like, dislike or demand and reject. Junk is one particular thing that very commonly and easily enter any house. Even if the parents put a ban on them, but still, they would easily and repeatedly enter through relatives, friends, neighbors or other cousins etc. Resistance against them, especially to keep the kids away will attract no less than a World War. As known fact, the junk is not just harmful but is also very dangerous. If that is the case, then how to keep our children safe and free from them?

Raja, who comes from a lower middle-class family, initially cannot afford for any extravagance. Paying the house rent, electricity bill, buying groceries and vegetables, paying school fee, buying uniform, stationery, the little one's milk and diapers, unexpected and sudden medical expenses can't give him strength beyond to afford on minting junks. The junk involves so much of hidden and untraceable cost. Once, habituated, then there's no easy end to control it. This is the reason secondary, but the primary for Raja is to impart a healthy living and healthy eating in his family. His son, who is into adolescence and daughter ready to wean and kick start play school have not been keen at the junk as yet.

How could they resist so well? How can that strict following of the parent's way of living sound pleasant and appealing to both of them? Firstly, Raja and Rani used to buy chocolates, biscuits or wafers on rare occasions, but in very little quantities. Secondly, they have requested visiting guests not to give them such things. Both the parents taught their kids so well that, even if someone gifts them these, they refuse to accept. And in case, if someone forces them in their tiny hands and pockets, they will give them to their parents and then forget. On rare moments, like school open days or holidays etc., a small amount of that food will be shared with the children. In such manner, both the kids adopted healthy living and healthy eating. No doubt, in the initial training, both of them made fuss to have the junk, but the strictness in the parents did not allow them to bow before the tantrums of the kids. After many trials, both of them learnt to accept the way it is going on.

Little patience, little endurance, little tolerance, little suffering can never disappoint you from achieving the aimed. There's plenty of life and abundance of resources in the days to come for munching and gulping the junk. But by then, one will come to a self-understanding of right eating. Keeping distance from them will give babies healthy teeth, systematic digestion, active mind, sound sleep. By doing so, harmful bulge, destructive shrink, improper growth and undesired sicknesses can also be prevented. Health and wealth, happiness and joy, abundance and insolvency are in man's own control areas.

No fortune, no favor, no inheritance can keep them stay with him forever. All that through the inheritance or fortune can just come to man, but keeping them live with him and keep growing is in his understanding and handling. More income cannot make one sufficient and rich, but the one who puts a cut at all the unnecessary expenses and adopts wise and calculative spending, in no time find great savings, abundance to keep them for future. Maintaining junking distance is then the mantra for healthy life and healthy finance.

Mantra 9

EXPENSIVE ARTISTS

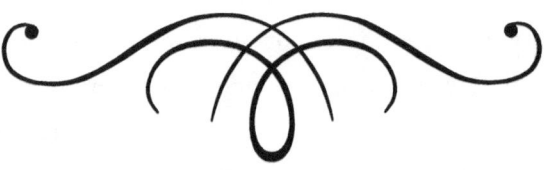

Denying our little darlings their desired and choicest favorites, squeezes our hearts to the point of bleeding. Some of their demands, though shouldn't be agreed upon, but the weak capacity to not able to say 'no' gives them the successful ride. Difficulty in differentiating, when to agree and when to be strict also puts the parents at many risks. The toddler and adolescent ages appear very sensitive, their tantrums seem to be okay and agreed. Their cries only mean 'yes' from parents and all others, even if it is actually a strict 'no'.

Parents therefore, confused, clueless and helpless, surrender before their little ones in many things. Once a surrender, is always a way and means for kids to get things on their side. Parents, usually don't realize that the child had adopted tantrum, fuss, cries as methods of being answered positively and get what they had determined. This continues to the teenage and further, and then the parents realize to put an end to this system. But by then, the child had adopted a different psychology and mindset. Breaking it would result in unpleasantness and distances at heart.

Children, whether small or big, always possess a curious mind. The new born too want all that catches their attention. They have a testing methodology, since they lack a firm grip in their tiny fingers, they immediately push those things to their mouths. They taste everything, adopt liking and disliking at particular things. Usually, they like thin and lighter objects, so that they can hold and play with them. Their curiosity to have such things and know them is basically risky. Especially the infants, even before attaining the age to hold a pencil or pen is strongly attracted unto them. Not many get involved in serious writing and learning before age, but they want to scribble their mind as it becomes a play for them. Seeing their enthusiasm, parents interfere to teach them the right way of holding pencil and learn alphabets and numbers. The fact is, they are least bothered to learn. They just want to run the pencil as they wish.

It is fine and good till here, even parents feel okay even when they insist upon a pen. When the parents use it or some elder sibling is using them, the little ones also desire that those writing tools should land in their hands. The problem for some begins here. They find that their little ones are using pens and running over themselves, parent's clothes, hands, legs, palms, feet, walls, bed sheets, pillows, furniture etc. But for others, saying no is getting squeezed at heart, and stopping them is not at all a thought to carry.

Pampering is not parenting, but spoiling. If one comes to an understanding of this, corrective and alternative measures by themselves will pop up in mind. Feeling mesmerized at the little finger's artistic zeal must be an instant emotion for everyone. But if the artist runs his/her pencil over the walls and the above listed surfaces instead of paper or canvas, then the vigilant teacher inside of the parent must step forward for swift alternate action.

Failing to teach the child the surfaces of writing and drawing, not able to stop from using the wrong ones, the parents are personally responsible for raising expensive artists. Giving the child instructions and sufficient papers for writing and drawing, with strictness, will save you thousands of rupees. Failing which, repainting of the walls, throwing away the ink-stained bed linen, costumes, and all other goods will incur additional expenses. Careful parents will dare to have white walls, wear white costumes boldly and stay fearless, even when their little ones are fiddling with the writing tools. Little caution, little resistance, little training, little patience will help you in decorating your walls and house with good interiors, even with delicate ones. Therefore, the mantra to have beautiful house in spite of having little kids is, 'give the appropriate writing surface with scribbling tools.'

Mantra 10

GREED AND THEFT

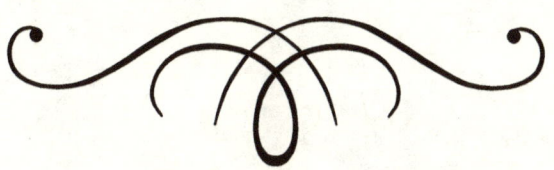

Satisfaction is a level, balanced, that people hardly try to attain. Saying 'no' seldom becomes tough, especially, when the demand for more is persistent. Only a sage, lazy or some ideologue is least worried about future and the fear of being unmet of daily adequate life. The craving for more in forms of food, money, wealth, clothes, jewelry, vehicles etc. may tend to break the line of discipline and proper way of getting them. This, if clearly visible or exposed, then embarrassment and discomfort will bring along shame and disgrace. Which, in turn can affect behavioral issues.

Infants and babies straight away attack and lay hands on any food plate they come across. They have no knowledge about the owner of the food. They can't either know anytime soon. For them, it is just food, attractive and appealing, and that is for eating. They even tend to fight and cry seeing eatables in other kid's possessions. But when it is about the one, for which they are the rightful owners, it is mostly next to impossible to have a tiny share from them. Parent's persistence to make them sharing, efforts to stop them from being drawn towards others plates usually go fruitless. Only achievement for them would be turning pink and blue with shame and embarrassment.

Teaching must begin from the very early days. This is what we have been learning and continue to stick to the same. When it comes to the point of food, the teaching follow sufficiency. Feeding the little ones with small portions, and very particularly the staple food at four intervals of the day, rather than two or three would keep them fill and away from want of more. As learnt, the junks in little proportions too at large intervals, only to give them the taste and feel of life would distance them from craving.

Teaching them to eat from their own plate, very strictly restricting them never to have from sibling's or parent's plates will discipline very soon. Doing this not only restricts them to stick to their plates but also enables them to know that it is wrong to even peek into others plates. Parents, who eat after feeding their babies or late, usually tend to shower their love at them by offering a bite or a morsel once again. This can never teach the baby to stop overeating, staring at others, crying, fighting for foods. This situation is more embarrassing than anything else.

Most parents complain of overeating in their kids. They get tired, frustrated but cannot help their little ones from being overweight and obese. Plump and chubby babies look cute and adorable, but parent's sense must rise from enjoying cuteness to keeping them healthy. Anything less or more is never healthy, so is eating. Healthy parenting involves balanced feeding and right feeding. Upon doing this, children can be very active and swift. They can be flexible and always on toes for energetic routines. As we are dealing with family below the middle-class status, where providing all these in sufficiency is practically impossible. But smart parenting can make this happen, let their children feel they have so much and everything. At the end we will learn the mantra to keep our little ones from greed and stealing.

When the child is not accessible to sufficiency and satisfaction, the craving demand by itself teaches him/her to pick up things without permission and without being noticed. This is robbery at home. Though, not a big offence, but in the future run will prove to be one. Hiding things, like food and money can never get control over the children. Letting them exposed to such things and teaching their value and the right ways of consumption and usage will spare them from placing hands unnecessarily.

Raja and Rani did the same with their son and daughter. Small, little things they would bring home, would announce with so big hype, letting the kids feel that it is not a mere cake but a very big thing. They used to teach their kids that how much efforts do the farmers, suppliers and retailers make, so that the food reaches the people. They would also let them know about their difficult days as kids. Most importantly, they make them have a sense that there's a majority of the world population, which doesn't find fortune for this food. They also make sure that the kids take part in the charity along with them, out of that little they have.

Coming to the point of money and teaching its value, this couple shares the details about their income, how and in what all their spending goes. While making purchases at the vegetable market, grocery store etc., Raja would prefer to get the change either in coins or smaller denominations. He would then go home and call the children, pouring out the coins in front of them, saying, this is yours. Then both the kids would distribute equally between them and put them in their kiddy banks. If some visitor or family members gift them any amount, Raja would ask them to put them in their piggy banks. He made savings accounts on both the little one's names in the bank. After a month or two, he would ask them to count and deposit them in the bank. Raja makes them to fill the pay in slips, cheques and also withdraw amount from ATM etc. Therefore, the mantra to keep the greed and theft away from entering children's minds is by sufficiency and satisfaction, even in little.

Mantra 11

WAIT FOR NO ONE

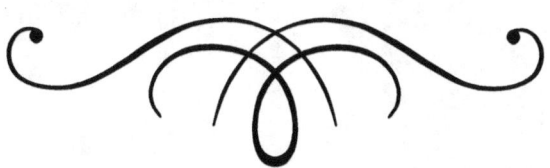

*T*ime and the world have their pace set. They move and function in the prescribed order. They see no one's face, they are senseless unto anyone's feelings. They are perfect and are at work all the time. They set standards and milestones for people to follow, but never take orders or instructions from anyone. They make the lazy active, the slow faster, the still to move, the sleeping to rise, the crying to smile, the sad to laugh, the sick to health, the ignorant to wisdom, the illiterate to literate, the unwilling to willing the disorder to order, the demons to depart and the God to appear.

They gave the requirement and the last person of the universe followed it. They appear beautiful and lovely only under favors. The blessed blesses them and the unfavored curses them. They don't mind because they have no feelings, emotions or life like humans. But they are the life and provide innumerable opportunities every day to live, make, remake, achieve, store, restore, replenish and revive. They are the bosses and everyone, from the king to the simple common man is their servant. They can never be wrong, but those that move against them are always and will always be wrong.

Raj Kumari was a lock down baby, so was Raj Kumar, making baby steps at school during the same period. It wasn't particularly for Raja and his family, but for the entire human race, it was a terrible hit all of a sudden. The existing at this day are fortunate fighters and grace filled ones to see the sun rise over them again and again. Millions were restricted for another sun and moon from welcoming them again. But the life at home in isolation wasn't easy for anyone, except for the rich, influential and powerful.

The middle class, lower middle class and the poor suffered very badly. The lives of the poor had no price at all. They were left to die on their own. Survival for the fittest truly came into effect during that period. If lives were lost due to the covid virus, then they were also lost due to starvation, cruelty of the administrations, negligence of the healers, lack of medicines, facilities, work force; fear, anxiety, loneliness, suffocation, mental trauma and the sudden bad news causing heart attack.

Death entered the lives of people and their houses mercilessly. It spared no one except the fittest and graced. Weeping and wailing was all over the earth. Some could get the honorable farewell at burial and cremation grounds. Some bodies did not reach either their beloved ones or even to the respectful last rites sites. Many were dumped, many were burnt without any intimation or notice to their people. Many places witnessed the flow of bodies on the river waters. Lot of the cremated and buried were still alive. Some of them could manage to get back home with the watchful help of the present people.

Terrific, horrific, inhuman and cruel was that period. No one was to be trusted, no one was to be approached too. Beyond this side of life, there was a wide range of humanity, charity, love, care and concern seen among many, who volunteered to help, save the lives. Thank God, that haunting moment turned out just history today, ending its deadly spell over the earth. May God never ever allow such times and instances to occur again! The suffered can only see the ghosts playing, the spared and the privileged can see God moving along.

Since, Raja and his family were part of this period, the couple took great care never to cause any harm hit them. The only option left before them like the whole world was remain indoors. Staying in that tiny part of the restricted world had not allowed many provisions, facilities, alternatives and choices. Since, Rani was good at food management and efficient to let her kitchen run smoothly even in little provisions, she took care of the family very well. Raja believes in self-disciplined and perfectly organized days and life. That made him prepare schedules of the day and engage all of them actively for right mind and joyful time. The family engaged in indoor games, chatting among themselves, taking out their talents of vocals, music, dance, acting, drawing, painting, window gardening, art and craft etc. That was especially a very blessed time for togetherness, if one longed for them. Ignoring the shortage of supplies and restricted movement outside, the rest for a loving family was all well.

Since, the government had released the text books online, Raja downloaded them and both the couple began to teach them periodically. Almost it was a school at home with parents as their teachers. The school calendar was strictly followed. In spite of being the entire day a holiday and indoors, the couple made it a point with their children to rise from the sleep as on regular working day and after full day's learning, working and pass time enjoyment would retire to bed early as usual. This family never tried to break the rule of routine for life, but instead practiced even when there was a choice not to be so particular and strict. Having a rule laid for themselves to distance from television, internet and gadgets, it neither hurt them much nor enslave them at that enticing period of life.

Few days passed, the school began online classes and both the kids got involved seriously. Raja had passed strict order to the kids, especially to Raj Kumar, 'never mind even if your entire class abstains from attending online and switching on their cameras. They might not even come on uniform, but you must be regular, attentive, well groomed, responsive to teachers with your camera on. Do prepare yourself for exam, even in case school may not conduct them. I want you to do it for yourself, not for others. The syllabus is meant for you to have an exposure to those areas of learning in every subject, including the languages. Learn them, excel in them, master them and define your life in your own way, right from this age itself.'

The rules and regulations at Raja's home would sound orthodox or more than strict discipline, at times when the entire world was in other words celebrating vacation during lock down at home. But that family did not mind others, instead followed their way of living according to the time and the world order. Since, they believe that anything that comes to man to keep him from functioning from normal and required way of living and moving ahead is a honey coated knife. That's the reason that family did not keep themselves at deception which might derail them from the complete system of living.

He continued to instruct his son Raj Kumar, 'do not be influenced and learn them, when friends or people around you do any wrong. Rather, learn and attain all that good comes in front of you, may that be any source. The time and the world wait for no one. They hold the same attitude towards you too. Be charged, be alive, be attentive, be yourself. Do not wait for time and the world to set the order on you. Reverse the order, redefine your time and create your world. Set your order before time and the world. Let them accept you and your doings. Let that be your order set for others.' The mantra to cope up in any situation and time is, 'wait for no one. Do it for yourself, do all that you can, and do it now.'

Mantra 12

THE SOURCE THAT SPRINGS

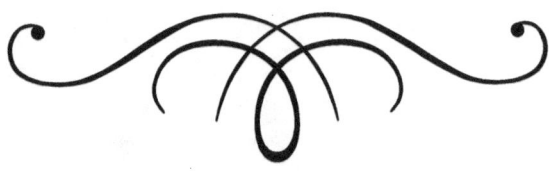

Regret should never visit people with exclamations of deep sigh. Sorry state must not occur due to personal errors. 'Wish it could have been otherwise,' must not be the results of future introspection. Failing to do right, to do good, to do more, to have more, to give more and to see it better would only increase the gap more in the vacuum, but can never fill. Careful thinking, proper planning, right implementation at the right time will never allow space for any regrets.

To have a regret free life, one must follow the principles of right living. They are not available freely everywhere. They ought to be searched diligently and learnt dedicatedly. They can be obtained from the wise people, who either made calculated steps initially or found them later from experience. Raja and his family provide the careful implementation of life's principles as they got them from the wise ones of the past. Raja is very particular to go on searching for pearls of value that impart wisdom upon him. He never misses any chance to learn and to train the same to his family.

Sometimes, situations and circumstances leave us at the parched lands with so little of sources and resources. But when life at those dry places demand for survival and sufficiency, then the discovery for sources and resources at other locations begins and compels to travel far in their pursuit. Finding them at distant lands if that is meant for survival, then storing the same and making your own land the resource center with abundance must be the next move for invention. Adjustment with little can keep the life cycle on move but filling the treasures with plenty for today and for tomorrow must be generation next goal. You cannot share what you don't have. You cannot show what you don't find. You cannot take to places that you haven't travelled. You cannot make others what you cannot be.

Raja and Rani couple have a son and a daughter. They are the apple of their eyes. They brought them into this world with so much of love and affection. They also are raising them with the same. They see that their home can never become a parched land, especially in terms of values of modelling themselves. The husband and wife share a very loving and respectful relationship. They have disagreements and sometimes disputes at petty levels, but that never takes a fight form.

In exceptional instances of heated arguments, they wait till they find home without children. They shout at one another, releasing the pressure out but finally come to either common agreement or to leave it for time to settle. They let the hypocrisy act well before the children on rare occasions of disagreement and dispute. They do this, so that their little hearts and minds don't have any hurting traces of life. It doesn't mean they don't show dissension appear before the kids. They do it very well, but not to the extent of calling it a fight or quarrel.

Both the kids were fortunate to see the abundance of love, care, harmony, friendship, goodness, gentleness, wisdom, knowledge and understanding available at home. They love to be in the company of their parents rather being with peer group other than the play time. The way their parents created the value system in the family, the kind of bond they share with them, the model of life they presented, the inspiration and motivation they laid in front of them, the wise way of handling difficulties and issues, the gentle dealings with all, the solutions for their challenges at the school and neighborhood etc. makes them their true role models and express their desire to be like them as they grow.

The kids had no fear of the future, since at first, they have their able parents to look after them very well in any given situation. Secondly, they have also enabled them to see the other side of life and face its challenges based on their learning. Both the kids are growing up in age, and well-mannered personality. They are studios and sincere at their responsibilities being students. They have adopted obedient and respecting mind set. They see all that expected from them being modeled before them. This made them return a pleasant and trouble-free life to their parents. Except for situational difficulties, nothing was there in the form of headache from their children.

If you are the dry parched land at value system, then your offspring can never be different from it. If you are the source and resource with abundance of life and all the good value system, then your offspring can be your treasure house and a spring of the same. Therefore, the mantra for a replica of your being to be seen in your offspring is, 'present yourself as the source and resource of all you want.'

Mantra 13

OUTSMARTING THE SMART

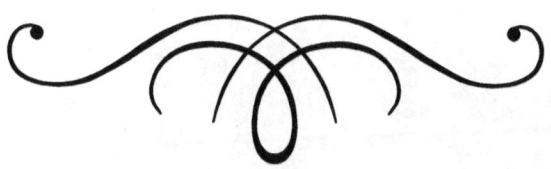

Changing time and the changing world order sets new formats and standards for the people to follow. Not everyone succeeds to pick up every change and every new definition. A very small percentage of the human world accepts every challenge of the world and outshines as triumphant. A little more of the same world sees itself reaching the set standards and changed challenges of every present era. Majority of the world population fail to even know, understand, grasp or attempt to see that as a parameter to reach and cross over victorious.

Every passing day has its splendid developments, all for advancement in every area of life supporting systems. Education, communication, medicine, agriculture, industry, trade, commerce, science and technology are some prominent aspects that keep advancing from time to time. The nature and environment in this due process develop hurting changes that yield hazardous, threatening and dangerous disasters. They appear in the form of global warming, climate change, earthquakes, floods and forest fire etc. Apart from these devastating disasters, like pollution in air, water, foods etc. too are slow poisonous changes that human life is hit all the time.

Living in the post covid era is not very easy for most population of the world. The advancement or paradigm shift in the area of communication demanded every illiterate to place himself in the race and learn internet language. This had not just dragged communication to internet waves but also every trade, education, petty sales and purchases. Man was forced to run with the pace of the world order. Failing which, only the individuals suffered, nothing happened to the world system and it's Implementors.

In every generation, the younger generation proves to be smart and advanced. The parent generation feels itself outdated, illiterate, ignorant of the world that its heir is born into and is living. The possibility for ill-treating the parents, considering them conservative, old fashioned, outdated and knows nothing kind of attitude develop in the children. If that is true with parents, then agreeing for every idea and decision of their children, either right or wrong will gradually take place. Many children in such cases takes their parents for ride, misbehave with them, insult them before others, make expensive decisions etc.

Not able to meet the advancing standards of the children, parents go helpless and face painful times all through. And when this happens, the grip of parenting that was firm so far begins to lose and every order disappears for drastic results. The wish to see our children smart must be the lovely wish of every parent, but being smarter than them must be their prime vision and aim as well. For that, parents must equally be literate and well qualified academically.

They must have knowledge of the subjects that their children are going through. They must possess the ability to be their teachers at home, efficient and advanced. They must at least be a graduate in some discipline. They should be spending time in front of their children in some learning or productive activity. Parents must not indulge in entertaining acts when their children had to be serious at studies. They must have entertainment time together as scheduled periodically. Seeing parents having pass time while they had to concentrate in studies will certainly distract their attention and result in poor grades.

Parents should never fall to such state where they don't have answers for their children's questions. Let them be from academic subjects, from the life and from every advancement. Updating oneself must be the motto to impart artful parenting. Seeing the world change, understanding its level, grasping its speed and depth, sharpening the abilities to learn, cope, excel and master them must be the burning fuel to ignite the life run and give it the driving energies.

An outdated and old-fashioned parent is always prone to ill-treatment. An earning, yet unlearned parent attracts no respect or little value. Strict but disorganized parent adds no weight to his instructions. A preaching but not practicing parent finds no proper landing of his views. A taskmaster but emotionless parent draws no love. Intelligent parent yet out of race from advancing world makes no room among intellectuals. The mantra to have a respectful, wise, acceptable, loving and honorable parenting is, 'make every effort to see your children smart and advanced, but also see yourself outsmarting every smartness in all respects.'

Mantra 14

RESPECTFUL LENS

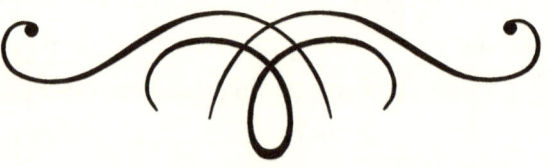

The world of a new born has very few members. And they are the parents, siblings and extended family members, if they are around. Though, the babies might be spending good amount of time with neighbors, visitors or relatives, but they would be spending quality time with the parents and siblings. All they have around them is their world. Their understanding, their foundation, their learning, their nature, character, their language, taste; culture and faith and religion, all comes from home.

In other words, parents are the eyes of their babies. They possess nothing of their own but builds themselves upon what their parents have seen, learnt and developed. Good and bad, right and wrong, moral and immoral all that a parent possesses, the baby is accessed unto. At some stage of life, the growing or grown-up child might begin to redefine his/her life, either from bad to good or vice versa. A parent then must be careful unto what he or she is up to.

The choice of a school and/or tuition is solely parent's. There could be advices followed or personal decision while enrolling their kids for learning. Some parents desire to give their children the best and prestigious institutions. While others would satisfy themselves for ordinary standards matching their financial capacities. Children at prestigious institutions might get low grades, those at ordinary standards may get high grades. The common expectation is contrary to this. Additional tuitions or special coaching may take birth due to low marks. In the past,

Artful Parenting had dealt with several reasons for poor marks. This mantra too will deal with another reason and solution. Since, the parent is the initial source of every vision and view point, then he/she must be having clear, right and respectful lens.

Parents of rich status, influence, powerful, political, poor mannered backgrounds etc. always try to make their presence and power known everywhere. They expect least actions of discipline over their children, but great results. Some of them even don't mind for any percentage of marks. All that they want is their children just attend school and pass out. Even if they don't pass, some have no concern at all. Such parents always interfere in school discipline and if needed tell their kids not to fear as long as their parents are there.

They speak bad words about the teachers, they demean the standards of the institutions, they disrespect the school authorities and teachers in front of their kids. Such parents do also speak ill about education and present it as inferior to money and wealth. They present bad and poor examples of the failed, who in spite of being a graduate is jobless. Parents of such attitude and character have no idea and are least bothered of the impact on their children. They are blind unto respectful side of life. Massive wealth, strong influence, powerful position in the society can result in full of arrogance.

Enrolled in any institution, irrespective of its performing standards, a good parent always raises its value and worth in the sight of his/her children. Such parents also show and teach their kids to respect their teachers and love the school they are studying. Sometimes, teachers might be wrong in something or the other, but still refraining from speaking bad against them and explaining to the children that it could be a mistake or error will keep them have reverence remained.

A wise parent knows that demeaning and disrespecting the teachers and the school of their children will help in no way but only will make way for poor standards. They also present the beautiful side of the life that they are to see and meet after sometime. Filling the lives of kids with sweetness and removing bitterness from the same, if entered in them through some source, should be the constant and only purpose of a caring and loving parent. Therefore, the mantra for marvelous results and amazing performances in all respects of life of your children is, 'have respectful lens and zoom well before them.'

Mantra 15

MORE GHASTLY THAN CIVIL AND WORLD WARS

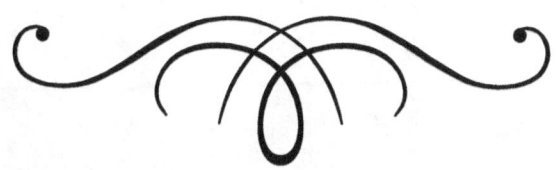

We are surrounded by around two hundred established nations, each with its unique nationality and power. Each nation again has many languages, cultures, traditions, customs, religions, faiths and practices. Almost each of the foresaid has something good and right to follow. Culture and tradition especially have basic foundational teachings that present reverence unto the elder generations. Some parts of the world even take to the extent of parent and ancestral worship.

The intent of such practices as part of culture and tradition is to impart the sense of belongingness and bind one another in relationships cords. This practice led to the survival of people as communities and colonies. The bond inside those particular communities grew stronger to the might of resisting outer forces of other communities. Each one tied firm in relational threads and lived intact within their established groups. With the rise of increased population, the geographical spread occurred horizontally. Small colonies and communities flourished vastly and spread across widely.

Travelling distances became part of life with the emergence of the need to connect from far and distant colonies. Multi cultured life for the travelers or migrants became a challenge. Adoption of little practices from other regions have diluted the sanctity and reverence of own culture and practices. The value system and family bonds too faced hurting affects, resulting improper behavior in the name of modernism. The value-based practices sound conservative and old fashioned. The love, affection and relational bonds are cornered for selfish and instant gains.

The life span in any relationship has been reduced to shorter terms. Inequality and divisions among the family members rose to unstoppable extents. The spread of various cultures, the adulteration of each culture, the vanishing and diminishing value system of life resulted in brokenness and loneliness everywhere. Thanks to those insolvents of right values, at least awoke to run back to reestablish the life's values, who once neglected and kicked out the value system, terming it meaningless and out fashioned. Such awakened parents are spending today thousands and thousands, days and years to learn right and bonding parenting.

Raja and Rani determined themselves to be exemplary parents for their children. They firmly believe that their sermons and sessions have no value and acceptance, unless they first make those demonstrating steps. Sibling wars, spouse wars, friends' wars, neighbors' wars, relatives' wars are more frequent and ghastlier than civil or world wars that takes place few times in the history. Battles at home are frequent and are almost daily. The poison that evolves inside the family is much greater than that being produced elsewhere throughout the world. But it is beautiful to see this poison destroyed through love, harmony, forgiveness and togetherness. Preventive way of living is always a wise man's choice. So are Raja and Rani. They made their lives and family based on strong principles. They have the control system installed and operated perfectly at every phase of life.

Building their complete beings on systematic, step by step analyzed and experimented way of calculated living, they decided to produce the bonding glue so abundantly, that everywhere it must be seen. This bonding glue keeps all four of them intact in one perfect circle. This glue is composed of love, respect, honor, sacrifice, sharing, caring, forgiving, helping, giving and encouraging. The parent couple always sacrificed their best for the sake of one another. So did they taught their kids to share and sacrifice. Their kids learnt to love and care the sibling. They practiced the acts that involve sacrifices. Their sense of belonging to one another produces joy in sacrifice than pain and grumblings.

Together as they are growing in age, both the siblings are growing in love and affection too. Their bond has reached to another level of maturity, where they don't require any more sermons on sibling love. Since Raja and Rani managed to live life free of spouse wars, family wars, neighbor wars, relative wars, friends' wars etc. they have succeeded to give their kids too, a life free of sibling wars and others. Both the kids have clean and cool nature. They are friends to all and enemies to none. The mantra to live a Life, free of all wars is, 'when every culture fails, make your own life an acceptable culture unto others. Produce so much of glue that everything everywhere and everyone every time is bonded with inseparable cords.'

Mantra 16

A STICK AND A MINUTE CLOCK

*E*very birth is not a planned one, neither is that a purposeful one. The births in this world, most are accidental, unwanted, hurting, shameful, insulting and painful. Nuclear families, unavailability of elders, lack of guidance and advice to the newly wed produces untimely generations. The desire or want to have a child has the primary purpose to produce an offspring, who will inherit their family and ancestral wealth and lineage. There's love, care, affection and proper way of handling among some unto their children, others mostly have a way of handling rough.

Some go beyond the extent of hard, harsh and cruel methods of handling their kids. All that is contrary to sensitive and delicate handling leaves hurting scars on the kid's hearts. Some of them develop traumatic experiences, feel scary even to the kind and loving closeness of their parents, elders. This happens because some people all of a sudden hit the children, without even hinting them that they are going to punish them for some cause. Having been through such sudden and cruel acts, the children can never develop a good and loving bond with parents.

A loving and caring parent doesn't spare the stick while disciplining the kids. But there's always a right way of handling or using stick. Children do make mistakes, wrongs, mischief. They may speak lies, steal, cheat, quarrel, fight, rebel, back answer, skip school, lag behind in studies, misbehave and disobey etc. This is quite common in most of the kids. Parents have their own ways of handling such behaviors.

Most of them use the stick, belt, ladles, sandals, boots, ropes etc., means of teaching them right ways. Such handlers let all their relevant and irrelevant anger fire on the backs, cheeks, hands and legs of their little children. Some go to the extent of locking their kids in homes, bathrooms, or keep them out of home as punishment. Many are such measures they adopt to teach their children to mend their ways and have right behavior. Though, these kinds of correcting ways may bring results in kids shun some or all wrong paths, but will also produce great amount of pain and suffering. Such methods cannot glue them with parents in love bond.

Raja and Rani too are parents of two kids, a daughter and a son. Those kids too had been through wrong behaviors. Many were the instances they had caused their parents to mad anger, and use stick on them to correct. But the parent couple never adopted any harsh or cruel way of beating, bashing and then correcting. They learnt to use the amount of anger in proper measures. They had never used it in excess and burst out with irrelevant anger. They ran stick on their children, but at the same time maintaining their dignity and also considering the delicate nature of the little ones, and they never gave anything beyond their suffering and coping capacities.

Soon after the use of the stick, the parent couple would reverse the minute clock and ask their kids to run into their laps before the last sand trap of the clock drops down. They first ask their kids to kiss them and they too kiss their kids saying, 'you did something wrong. The stick that ran over you was your punishment. Now, it is over. Hope you learnt where you went wrong. Don't repeat it again. Understand?' The kids answer positively and promise not to repeat it ever. Then the whole family forgets all that and get involved in happy talk, laugh and joyful in something else.

The set principles and rules of the family at first instance doesn't provide room for any misbehavior. Secondly, even if any wrong, mischief, fights, in and out of home or anything else happens, then the kids were given boldness and confidence to report them to parents. By doing so, the parents assured them that they would never be punished. Failing which, even if it was a small thing, but they will be punished. Therefore, the kids were never found with any scary or traumatic behavior. The right and loving way of disciplining them had developed great amount of respect and bonding emotion unto their parents. The mantra for a healthy, fearless, affectionate parenting is, 'always use a minute clock, when needed to run a stick over your children.'

Mantra 17

TROUBLE SHOOTING

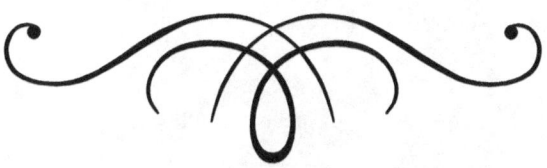

Give, keep giving or give and take, or take, keep taking is the everyday business of all the existing humans on the face of the earth. There's no limit and dearth for the billion things, ideas, thoughts that go into exchange around the clock. The nature and creation too participate in this act. It responds and returns back in multiple folds for what you have desired and demanded from it. It keeps on giving, it also returns back on what you give.

There's only one store house that measures larger than any other visible and invisible place in this universe and that is the human brain. This sends signals, clear directions, understandable commands and agreeable or disagreeable wishes. This in turn also receives infinite number of materials that etches in the memory for short and long terms. Every signal, thought or idea has working effect, beneficial, harmful, troubling, helpful, constructive or disastrous. Some give pleasures, some happiness, some education, some thrill, some entertain, some sadden etc., to the extent of helplessness.

Not every signal is good, not every feeling is right to be felt, not every thought is healthy, not every idea is to ponder and is to be accepted. Not every sharing is worth receivable, not every person is a well-wisher, not everyone is clean in intention, character, behavior and nature. When the exchange is involved with good and bad, the discerning and judgmental capacities of an individual must function to perfect levels of wisdom and understanding.

This comes with age, maturity, learning, practicing and with developed good character. This learning and inspiration occur right from the very tender ages. One should have access to right and well-wishing people around them. If they are the caring and loving parents, then that individual is the most blessed and fortunate one. But this too is rare, because of lack of understanding parents, lack of ability and interest to teach, lack of the responsibility sense to be their children's first teachers in all respects.

Having the television on; mobile, computer or laptops running various entertaining programs, could be movies, movie songs, other songs, serials, commercials in the intervals, containing romance related talks, music, inappropriate dressing, adult related topics, commercials etc. pose several questions and feelings over the minds of all, especially the very little infants, adolescents, teens and also youths. Parents ignorant or careless about this impact on their kid's brains and hearts never mind to have censorship in their interests.

Kids keep growing with those thoughts and feelings in them. They might share with other friends or someone else about those strange feelings and troubling visions. In that exchange, if some wrong idea, thought or advice takes place, then the kid or growing kid might begin enjoying and playing with those feelings. This would result in attraction towards opposite sex even before they attain puberty. Many parents, schools and societies face this challenge and are troubled to handle their little ones right from the adolescent age itself. Confused elder generations have no clue other than punishing the kids and restricting them with strictness and warnings.

Raj Kumar and Raj Kumari reached their puberty state. Their well-trained, cautious, wise and responsible parents equipped themselves with stage-by-stage parenting. They knew to impart apt education at appropriate ages. So was about the physical changes their kids developed as part of growth process. Children find themselves caught up in fear and anxiety as they observe sudden and gradual developments.

The world usually counts this as one of the greatest days of celebrations. The Asian continent has several rituals, practices and celebrations, both for girls and boys. They arrange grand functions and invite large number of guests, friends and relatives. People pour in, some places for days, some for hours of celebrations. The confused child has no idea other than seated on the stage, receive gifts and appear special. The physical and mental changes continue to haunt the child, but she/he may not find anyone to help her/him out.

Raja and Rani did not go as per usual customs and culture. Instead, they sat with their children and educated them well that this stage is the beginning of entering into another age level called teenage. They explained them that they had already crossed over infancy, toddler age, adolescence and now entered teenage. They took away all their fears saying, it is neither strange, unusual nor anything to be worried about.

The kids learnt that they must maintain their personal hygiene and specially to free themselves from unwanted hair growths at private areas. They also were taught that with this physical change there will occur some confusions in emotions and feelings, but they are to be diverted, forgotten and replaced with right and useful thinking, involving themselves actively doing something. Those kids got the proper instructions to respect their bodies, honor the mind space with healthy thoughts, and never to play with any wrong thought, idea or feelings.

Talking to the kids about the puberty matters, personal hygiene, keeping them from strange feelings and acts is nightmarish for most people. Raja and Rani decided to break that wall of uncomfortable feeling, defeat the embarrassment while speaking to their kids, only with the fear and caution, if they fail to teach right, some others might teach their children wrong. As parents, they are not into any kind of entertainment or activity that may introduce adult content or talk to their children, and therefore, their children are safe and secure from watching and learning indecent, immoral or enticing things.

Both the parents gave censorship to their kids right from their toddler ages. In any case, by any chance, if they come across something wrong, the kids were told to close their eyes, divert themselves or move away from there. This led the kids to differentiate between the good and the bad, moral and immoral at the very young stage. As they grew in age, the parents were freed from such exercises because the foundation was laid strong in their kids. The mantra therefore, for clean and upright upbringing is, 'talk the hard talk, though it is hard to start. Be the trouble avoider, if needed be the trouble shooter.'

Mantra 18

THEY WON'T COME BACK AGAIN

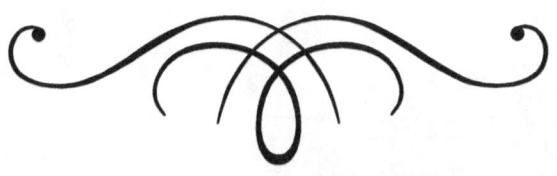

Traveling freaks discover so many things that any other ordinary person would ever do. They find many interesting and useful things, related to their journeys, for usage, for consumption, for experiences. They do own many things and have a special and vast collection. The most important and primary one that they would keep discovering, updating, modifying or replacing is their travel bag. Every traveler wishes to have compact baggage but at the same time want it to accommodate many things. This process has defined, redefined the single compartment rectangular, square boxes, cylindrical bags to multi partitioned stylish, compact, lightweight, easy to carry packs. This invention has benefitted everyone in several ways. This is known as 'all in one, always with one.'

The inventions and discoveries of the world too have been reshaped and resized, redefined and redesigned into macro and micro formats. The small tiny thing carries so much of information, material and empty space that millions of similar sized, types of other things can still be accommodated, restructured, modified, repaired and remade within themselves. This advancement has added so much of accessibility to various things of the world. Every change, transformation, advancement, creation and recreation of the world is solely due to the advancement in human brain. As the man's brain keeps advancing, innovating and discovering, the worlds and all that are in these worlds too get the actual shape from virtual shape, initially developed in man's brain.

The brain/reasoning has its expanding capacity, so is the memory. The brain has no limit in matters of thinking, creating ideas, learning and teaching. The memory space too is limitless to store anything that the brain either develops within or adopts from outside. The brain has the capacity to learn and understand anything and everything, visible and invisible, existing and even nonexistent things or ideas. This brain then can help man, his reasoning, his usage, his dealings with all that is needed for him anytime. The brain, if exposed to limitless learning and usage from very first days of babies' lives, then the intellectual and informative capacities of the same would make a mesmerizing wonder. The exposure towards various skills and abilities from infancy days can produce another wonder of the world.

But sadly, not many parents have this understanding. Not many are dedicated and interested in imparting activities that would put their little one's brain at work and for future advancement. Almost all the parents simply wish their babies play, sing, dance, run, jump, hop, skip, ride, crawl and squat. Some parents do buy educative toys, but they won't spend qualitative time with their kids. Many parents wish to present their babies to the world as learned ones, even before enrolled in play school. Such people teach alphabets, numbers and few things, but gradually that zeal and commitment diminish in them. They feel the rest of teaching or educating responsibility lies on the school and teachers. From this point, they simply satisfy themselves to see their kids fulfil academic learnings and assignments.

Raja and Rani are somewhat different from the majority and place themselves in the minority of the minorities. Their thinking and style of functioning does not match with many. They in one way have provided access to their kids to all the playful, happy and enjoyable childhood, but at the same time equipped them with mature understanding. The kids at young age rose to decision making stages. The parents involve both the kids in family discussions and decisions. The kids may be sometimes different but are not entirely wrong in presenting their ideas and decision making. They were left to volunteer themselves regarding the matters of school that involves their choice and decisions, particularly like the extracurricular activities. The parents have given them freedom, at the same time set instructions too, that they should never step back in any of the participation outside academics.

Encouraged and supported by the parents, both the kids found themselves exposed to many skills and abilities. They participate almost in every contest, race, competition, tournament, concert and stage. They came out with many medals, trophies, certificates and awards. They did not stay away from the Olympiads, scholarship tests and out of school participation. The parents made their kids understand that, all they do, learn, get and achieve is solely for them. Their success would remain with them forever. It would encourage and motivate them for greater attempts and achievements.

The parent couple makes it a point to be the first in the front row gallery of the audience or spectators. They make their kids feel good with their presence and encourage them for best performances. Upon failure, poor performances or difficulties, they would celebrate their day very special and motivate them to leave that behind and move ahead for the next participation.

This helped the kids to never feel bad but only to learn from the past mistakes.

The parents saw that their children should never feel bad for not having something or the other. When the kids have to be with the peer groups and it involves some price, they would not hesitate or rethink but would first make the payment, be it for picnic, tour or special camps. The parents feel that, if this opportunity is missed away for any reason, the thrill, joy, excitement, and happiness that would have produced great memories would also have been missed. They consider their kids and themselves as their complete world. And they would do anything and everything that makes their space beautiful and joyful. Therefore, the mantra for limitless and endless gains is, 'provide all that is due, for the history can never become present'

Mantra 19

EMPTY BAGS

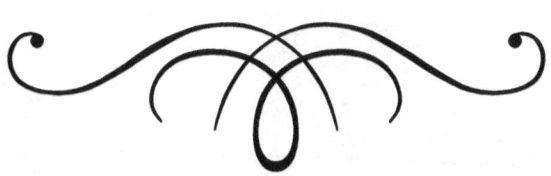

When the analysis on man's lifetime sufferings and the reasons for his punishments are summarized, then the innocent proves to have been blamed, accused and had wrongly borne everything because of his innocence and ignorance. But the naughty, mischievous, undisciplined faces them due to his own faults and wrong doings. Sometimes, the latter also suffers because of others plotting against him.

Some happenings could be unavoidable, some inevitable, some unknown, some even may mysteriously take place. There's no one who had never suffered, and there won't be anyone without having suffered for own reasons or due to others reasons. Being vigilant, wise, staying away from the vicinity of any wrong happenings and wrong doings, keeping oneself safe and secure from being risked must be one's main focus of trouble-free and remark-free life.

Raja Kumar and Raj Kumari are taught the same since their infancy days. They were told never to get involved in quarrels and fights, both at home and outside of it. They were educated to maintain the same at school too. When it comes to the point of having friends, their list must keep on added and go to limitless extents. And when it comes to the list of unwanted, disliked, hated enemies, their list must always stand at zero, complete blank.

The kids had and have been facing uncomfortable moments with several, at school, at other classes, at neighborhood and sometimes between them as siblings too. But the parents taught them to see the cause for such situations, understand why others did like that with them, 'let them know you don't like this, you are not comfortable with such kinds of behavior and talks. Once, twice or thrice, you may need to let your friends and others know what makes you comfortable and uncomfortable. Then, the situation will soon come into your control and in your favor.'

The kids understood this because they have adopted a different discipline from the beginning. Gradually, they had made friends with likeminded. Some naughty and mischievous friends too found place in their circles, due to the seating arrangements in school, and having made friendship with friends of friends. Parents keep a regular watch over their entire behavior and talks.

The kids were found using censored words at home, they were doing the same at other places too. Parents knew the reason for that bad development, and that was, because they didn't know that those are restricted and forbidden words. So, lovingly they made them understand why they are not supposed to learn and use such words. The kids heard someone use them frequently, and they have no idea about any restrictions and prohibitions in the usage of words. The parents do regularly keep inspecting them of what they have learnt, if by any chance adopted unacceptable behavior or talks.

Speaking lies, hiding facts, stealing, fighting, quarreling, hating, abusing, gossiping against others etc. are strict prohibitions at home and are check list items to be interrogated at regular intervals. The parents would sit with them and discuss, who their close friends are, how their friends are, who is naughty and mischief in their class. They sometimes throw arrows in the air and they would hit at the right target. Something like, 'why was teacher angry at you today, why were you punished, why did the principal summon your class today' and so on. The kids would always wonder how their parents knew all these. Who might have told them?

Then parents would respond, 'since our hearts always go after you, we will come to know even the silliest things happening with you.' The kids then pour out all that happened. The kids sometimes reported that they were commonly punished because of others mischief. Sometimes they had suffered in order to save their friends. The parents cautioned them for the first reason, 'anytime you are individually summoned, you should come out clean.' For the second reason the parents appreciated to stand for their friends, saving them from being punished. 'You shared their portion of punishment. It is also good. But you should attempt to make your friend aware not to behave wrongly, and if that repeats and becomes their habit and character, you won't be standing for them ever.'

In every parent and teacher meet at school, the parent couple always makes it a point to find from the teacher how their children are faring, in studies and personal conduct. The teachers always appreciated them in both respects, and assured the parents that they are the best. Despite of this, the parents would enquire about their behavior. And to let them know, if for any reason they have a complaint against them. Responding to the appreciation for academic scores, the parents divert the credit in their children's favor, saying, 'they are aware and concerned about their duties; they voluntarily prepare themselves for the academics and did well in exams. We did nothing, just monitored and guided them.'

As part of regular inspections and interrogations, both the kids are asked to present their books, other stationery and empty their bags. Then are strictly told to be careful and watchful of all their possessions. None of them should be missing ever. The usage of pencils, erasers, pens, books must be appropriate, they should be careful in handling them. Though extra pencils, pens and erasers are always with them, but the reporting with accountability would avoid any misuse, loss or carelessness.

Once, both the kids were found with others pencils and erasers in their bags on different occasions. The parents before enquiry gave small beatings on their small hands and asked strictly, why and how they entered their bags. One said, 'I found it orphan without any owner, it is a different color and design. I liked it, so kept in my bag.' The other said, 'I have no idea how it came into my bag. Trust me, I did not steal from anyone. I am truly innocent.'

The parents advised and cautioned them, 'firstly, you should always check whether all your belongings are there or not. Secondly, you should see whether others items have found place in your bags by any chance. Thirdly, whether anything lies orphan without an owner, you must handover it to the teacher, he/she will find its owner. Even if it is so fancy and attractive, you should not fall to its temptation. Any such liking unto anything, you can let us know, we will buy them for you.' The mantra to gift risk-free, remark-free and trouble-free disciplined life is, 'save the children from false traps, empty the bags.'

Mantra 20

HOLISTIC I LOVE YOU

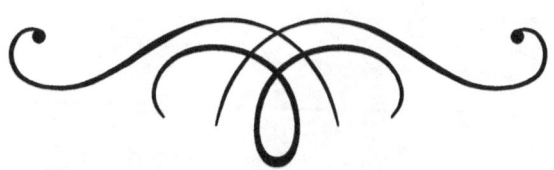

Signals produce themselves as preexisting evidences of the soon to be or later happening events, sometime in the short or long future. Some events die before taking place, so do the signals die with them and won't pop up again. As long as the future happening event keep taking shape inside the mind, the signals too will continuously be sent out; deliberately for the open activity, subconsciously for the secret agendas. The signals are the pressures produced as the reaction of any thought, which basically intends to do something. These pressures can't be withheld inside by the loose tongued, gossiper, showman; in other words, poor controlled.

The history proves that even the highly learned, well and carefully planned, very strongly controlled, secret worker cannot succeed in stopping the signals, that turn as clues and evidences to trace the roots. For any device to work, there should be both the signal transmitter and its receiver. The absence of either of them will not produce desired function. We are surrounded by thousands of different waves and signals, that are caught by the receivers and convert into bandwidth. Today, each and everything is based on these waves and signals.

People should be smart, vigilant, educative to read the wrong signals and stop any untoward happenings occur. Smart parenting involves reading the actions, knowing the hidden reasons behind each curios or casual question, statements and comments made on the behavior of others etc. Kids are full of curiosity, so is almost everyone who wishes to get to the knowledge of everything unknown, unseen, unheard and unexperienced. The same curiosity leads to several questions in the growing kids. They may ask about the forbidden and prohibited too.

Such questions will keep on arising as long as they don't come to the knowledge that differentiates 'the permitted and the forbidden.' Out of innocence they do send signals of their desires to experience the prohibited substances like tobacco and alcohol; matters like love and romance. The law of the land had set maturity, eighteen years as the eligibility to approach the so far restricted substances and matters, qualified to participate in anything as an adult, including the grant to drive, right to vote and choose their favorite leader etc.

The law withdraws itself from anymore custody, barring the parents too accountable along with it for the safety and security of the child after completing seventeen years. From there on it authorizes the child to get involved in any adult related substance or matters legally allowed. Consumption of tobacco, alcohol is not a crime after becoming adult. Getting involved in the boy and girl relationships, marriage without parent's consent is encouraged authorizing them as adult and free citizens.

But for the parents, these are the matters of serious concern and involve right and wrong morals. None of the parents wish their children enter into any of these and spoil their lives. Few are the guidelines to handle such instincts preventing birthing in their hearts, addressing that curiosity, killing or diverting that desire if at all taken place sometime ago or long back. One, tobacco and alcohol consuming parents cannot stop this catching their children. Because they have shown them the way, gave access, and above all are not concerned about their children to stay away from this. Those teetotaler parents need to check the signals the kids sent by the way they hold the pen, pencil or drinking glass. The cinema or somebody in the family might have left that fascinating feel over them.

Educate them that, since they are the harmful substances, so are they prohibited for consumption too. Those who are not bothered about their health, image as a good person acceptable unto all, will consume them at their own risk and loss. That is not the symbol of grownups or socially glorified as wrongly presented by cinema and the world. If needed, they should be warned to face punishment for going against the moral standards set by the family. The family that doesn't provide any discussions, pictures, any such substances, keeps their children from friends involved in them, is safely and securely confident that their children are free from being exposed into any addictions.

Two, the parents that glorify themselves of having love marriages, feeling proud to have gone against the wishes of all and got married, and keep them alive in all their discussions and talks; as stated above, are least bothered about their children entering into any relationships even before the legal age. Such parents even if try to control their kids by any chance, won't find value to their discipline, since they are preaching contrary to what they practiced and boast upon. But others might handle them wisely and tactfully.

The example of Raja and Rani as ideal parents leave many tips before the challenged parents. This parent couple found the curiosity in their children with indirect questions, mentioning them as their friends' not theirs. But the kids know what they were asking was not at all practiced by their parents at home, neither had they ever made access to romantic cinemas or literature. In their talks always there was respect for every relationship. There was holistic atmosphere in every bond they shared, between themselves as spouses, among the siblings, unto their parents and elders, even unto them as their parents. But still, since they have access and confidence given by the parents to approach them for anything, that may embarrass them later, they can find it from them.

The kids asked them whether it is wrong for a boy and girl to exchange the 'I love you' words. The parents asked, why did such question come into their mind. They said, it is not their question, but in response to what happened in the school. A boy said 'I love you' to a girl, and that was taken to the notice of the teachers. The school then called the parents of both of them. Now, everybody was discussing about the same. This had spread to many boys and girls and they too feel like doing the same.

Parents did not give them the straight answer as in the case of educating against other curious subjects. Instead, they asked them to go to bed for now, not to go to school for three days, wake up late in the morning, enjoy playing, going out, no need to study these three days. They told them to enjoy their time. They will give the answer to that question only after three days. Kids have no idea why the parents asked them to keep aside their school, studies but just to do nothing and enjoy.

As usual they sang praises, read the scriptures and said night prayer, good night and I love you to another. This is the holistic I love you that they practice from the very first day as a family. The exchange of the same occurs among all of them for several reasons in daily life. The mantra to present good examples against forbidden love is 'demonstrate holistic I love you.'

Mantra 21

TIME FOR SAYING I LOVE YOU

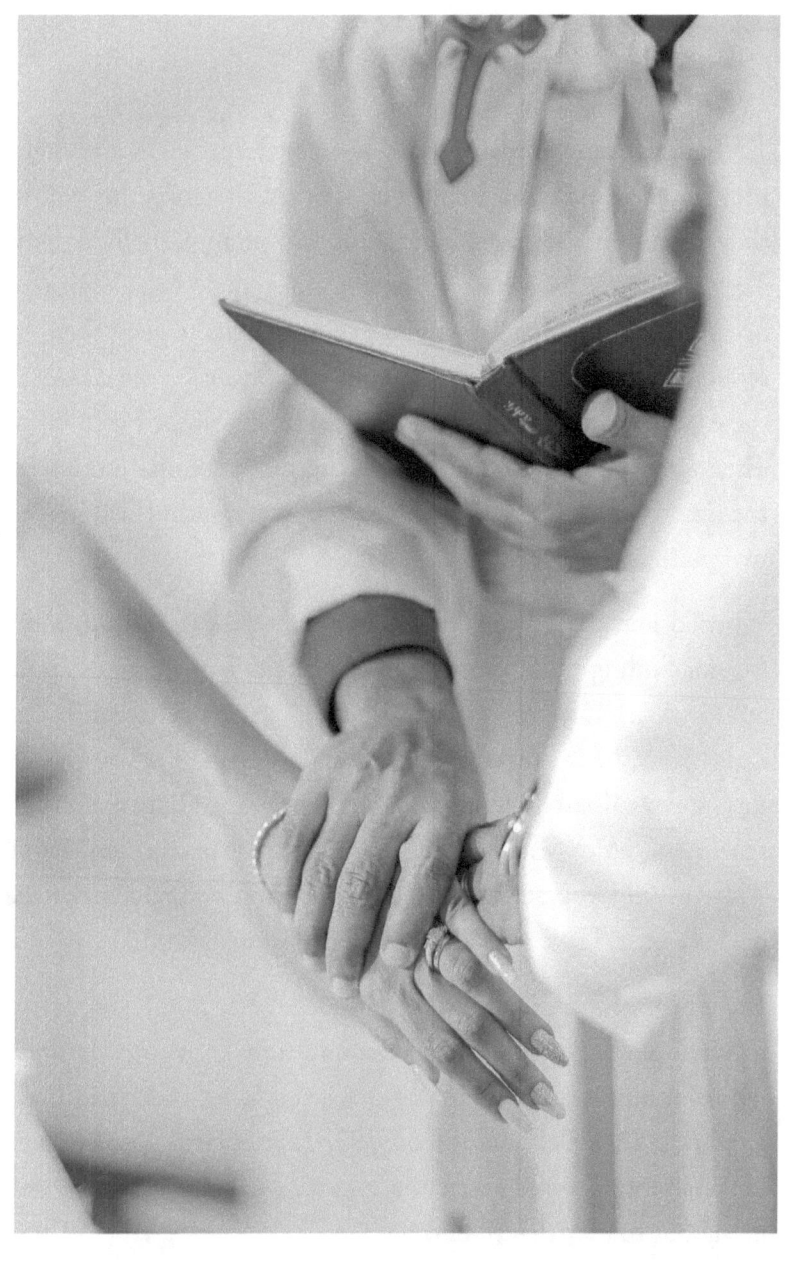

The kids went to bed but did not get sleep. The entire night they stared at the ceiling, and at each other. In whispering voices, they discussed the parent's reaction and strange methodology. They have no idea what's going on. They shared one another's opinion, and decided to convince their parents to send them to school in the morning. They cannot afford to miss the classes as the exams are nearing. Somehow, they finally slipped into sleep. Their alarms did not sound, so they did not wake up on time. By the time they came out of their sleep, the school time had moved two periods ahead.

Worried and disturbed kids found themselves in more trouble for not finding their parents at home, instead they found a note left for them. It stated, 'good morning kids, we have to move out early today. Your breakfast and milk are waiting for you on the dining table. Lunch too is ready and kept in the kitchen. You can reheat and enjoy your meal. We will be back by evening. Hope you will find yourselves relaxed in playful mode and make the best use of it. Have a good day ahead. Love you both.'

Except for both of them, there's no-one else at home. They tried to have good time at the playground and park, but returned within minutes, since there's no one around. All their friends are at school. The neighbors and others in their society posed strange looks at them, some asked the reasons for being at home and going out to play in school time.

They felt uncomfortable, unpleasant and bored at home. Their entire inner self is moving at school, though they are bodily moving at home and around. They could not enjoy their free day, even though all their desired are with them, because they felt that they have got all the right things in wrong time. Not knowing what to do, they simply spent time together playing, chatting and surfing the net. They eagerly waited and wanted their parents to return home soon.

By evening, the parents made their way back home. Greeted them with love as usual and with open arms for a big hug. The kids ran fast into their embrace and hugged them tight. The parents could feel the tough time they had at home. As they refreshed soon, asked their kids to get ready to go out for a good dinner. The kids swiftly got ready and are waiting at the door to step out. The entire family moved onto a good ride and found themselves at a good restaurant. They enjoyed their favorite delicacies and did not wish to miss the good time. After having their bellies filled, they hit the road to get back home. After sometime they are in their sweet heaven and slipped into comfortable home dress. As daily routine, they sat for prayers and then for a family talk.

The parents asked them, how was their day. They said, 'except for the one with you in the evening, ride and dinner, nothing else was fine. The entire day was suffocating and boring. It almost killed us badly.' But the parents asked, 'you have no responsibilities, no studies, no homework etc., but only to enjoy your whole time with your favorite pastime activities. Then why didn't you enjoy?' Their answer was, 'we got our favorite pastime liberty at the wrong time. We understood that right thing at wrong time can neither satisfy us, give us the thrill, nor is right.'

Parents wanted their kids to know and understand the same. They wanted their kids to learn this by themselves. The day off from school was just a demonstration but not punishment. At first point, since the kids haven't done anything wrong, so there's no point of punishing them. Secondly, since their kids were important for them, and keeping them away from any wrong tracks was high priority to them. Therefore, educating them through any means is their serious concern. The kids too understood what their parents longed to teach them. Since their kids' hearts are connected with their parents, they never felt bad for any of their sermons, demonstrations, corrections, preventive warnings too. They responded and reacted well with respect.

Parents explained their kids, the words 'I love you' are the expressions of heart to heart. There's holistic sense that could be shared with anyone, as we all do in the family. Among the good friends too this is holistic, between the spouses too this is the same. This can be openly said before anyone, in response to any favor, cooling the anger, getting the things done etc. Beyond this, the same could be expressed in private in the legal wedlock.

As you have seen that there is no joy for doing right thing at wrong time, getting into boy and girl relationship before the legal age and attaining full maturity, before acquiring right knowledge and understanding about marriage, before finishing studies and settling in career, this will nowhere produce the real joy and right results. Having the heart divided and shared to a boy/girl will only give the force the mind and brain to work for wrong means, which in turn will ruin the entire focus of the present and the future.

Kids got the complete understanding and assured their parents never to deviate themselves from the primary focus, and if at all they find anyone attracting them, as per the confidence provided by their parents, they will let their feelings known to them first. That is secondary, the primary promise they made was, they will keep themselves never fall to any such temptations, even though it looks fancy and attractive; and regretful in case of a miss, but still, they will hold their horses until they settle in life.

The mantra and educating the right time to say 'I love you' is, 'teach them the right time for right things. Give them the confidence that your kids must find a loving and understanding friend in you. They should find you the first person to come and report each and every good and bad feel at heart, mistakes or blunders and wrong doings. They should also find you as the trustworthy and confidential person with understanding and cool heart.'

Mantra 22

CORRECTING THE MEMORIES

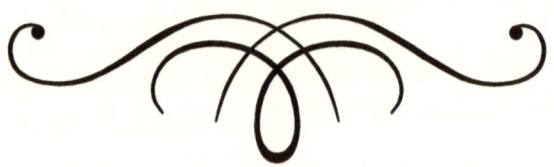

*E*very produced, seen, heard, felt matter makes its way straight into the memory lane and occupies the place allotted to it. Sometimes, it gets lost in the busy rush, jammed traffic of various happenings at the same time and fails even to make its way to the entrance of memory bank. Many a times, it finds the reverse path and escapes from the grip of the brain. The only things that remain firm in the brain, etched or engraved are the ones that are so much dear to heart, interesting, fascinating, relevant in day-to-day life, learnt with much efforts; painful, hurting, insulting, losses etc.

Apart from those with high values, both in good and bad senses, all others irrelevant and least important cannot etch or engrave themselves into the brain walls. It doesn't mean they are completely lost, perhaps they are somewhere in the same area but needs others or situations help to return back to the active and projecting area of memories. Sometimes, even the dead memory cells can also be brought back to life. If they are good, then can be made best use of them, if they are bad, they will play to ruin everything.

Every thought, idea or matter will convince man to act upon them. A bad one keeps on compelling until it loses its power against resistance. It doesn't accept defeat so easily; it will never give up unless it is chased out with strong and right character. But the battle would be fierce, constant, disturbing, troubling, hurting and expensive. This battle would devour lot many things if not defeated right in the very beginning.

In the kids, their innocence, good character, truthfulness, honesty, transparency; learning, grasping, reasoning, memorizing, retaining, logical, creative and innovative capacities and zeal are robbed. They fail to see the expected far from their reach, gradually categorize themselves in the company of ordinary grades and develop sour grapes mindset. The pain, shame, heartaches to both parents and kids is felt upon the reverse of expected results. The primary concern and goal of every parent is to see their kids perform well and top the ranks always. Anything contrary to this is real hell unto all.

Correcting memories comes into effect at this point. Careful parenting not only involves correcting punishment, warnings, but also correcting bad memories and erasing them. This is not an easy task, at the same time, it is not an impossible one too. As always said, little patience, little care, lots of time spent together and guidance provided, this can become mission accomplished. Parents need first to model themselves in all that they wish to see in their kids. They need to be honest, transparent, truthful and well mannered. The kids ought to sit and talk with parents as the first and the best friends. They should see fearlessness and liberty to discuss casually. They should be loving to spend time at home, involve in close relationship with one another rather than going out seeking others to speak their heart out. Parents who keep seeking privacy always drive their kids out and allow them to spend lot of time. This would allow exposure to outside world and it's matters. Then the parenting involves many challenges, present and the flood that will follow thereafter.

Raja and Rani presented their married life as the most honorable of all. The love and respect between them never presented any wrong impression over their kids. They have controlled all their feelings unto each other very well and managed to have a firm grip over them, never to miss out as a wrong behavior. They mentioned their love and affection in front of their children in holistic and respectful ways, in forms of words and actions. Their closeness before them was never mistranslated by the kids. Their dealings and handling of situations always gave their kids confidence and courage. Their corrections and punishments never hurt them to the extent of feeling bad. Because, they wouldn't keep that in mind for more than sixty seconds and also would never allow their kids to think and feel about it beyond that same limit. Therefore, the kids too never go to any extent of getting punished.

The best and the only way the parent couple found to correct their kids' bad memories is, firstly explaining what is right and wrong. Secondly, letting them no room for thinking about that matter. For this they would load their schedule with so packed events, that they hardly find any idle time. Thirdly, they involve them in regular day to day healthy and happy talks. Fourthly, they would drive them through Holy Scriptures and educate the moral and holy values. Fifthly, they would keep a check over their friendship and if needed restrict their movements in wrong company. The fully loaded day, healthy atmosphere at home, restrictions against meaningless and corrupting activities are the repairing tools for correcting bad memories. Therefore, the mantra for a good behavior, excellent and beyond expected results with exposure to various marvelous worlds is, 'correct the bad before it etch or engrave itself as bad memory and convert it into a conduct or behavior battle.'

Mantra 23
ORBITAL ORDER

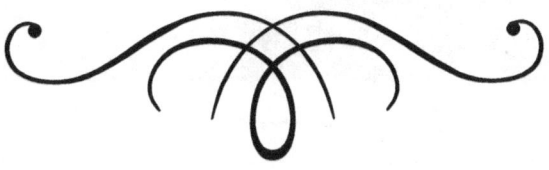

The species of animals, birds and sea creatures count innumerable when compared to the human race. Though each man may be different in stature, complexion, language and culture, but human race is the one and only compared to the former having unique identity in all forms. Whereas the rest of the species are entirely different from one another. Though the animal world is so vast in number, the human world is the only one that has the strength, capacity, wisdom, skills and abilities to make this world. The rest live in what was created, recreated, arranged, shaped and organized by humans.

The animals and birds though can only live in groups, but they cannot make colonies and societies unlike humans. They cannot produce anything other than their own species in reproduction. In some cases, they can only create food for humans. Apart from that, their contribution in making this world is nothing. Everything that was, that is and will be, is the handicraft of human race. Animals and birds are not bound to one another in long relationships. Their parent child relationship ends once the baby generation is grown up to independent stage. Their memories end with that, and there never exists any trace of this relationship. They become one in that common world. They do share certain emotions but not any relationships.

Relationships are seen only in humans. They vary in nature and fall into the categories of inseparable, separable and commons. People who fall in the category of inseparable extend a guarantee to see it unbroken. They promise to stick to their word and bring God, their deities, nature or people they love most and swear on their names. Not everyone keeps this promise or tries to keep it; they neither care to keep it nor care to try to keep it. The relationships that fall under this category are, spousal, parental and sibling. The first one comes from choice, the second and third comes as a result of the first choice.

Children are born to the spouses and they become siblings. No child has a choice to select their parents and siblings. They come into their lives without their consent. They have a choice either to make that bond strong and carry it forward as long as they live or break it any moment. But the people of this inseparable bond must be the responsible and volunteers to maintain their meaning, sanctity and strength unbroken. There could be conflicts, quarrels and fights in these bonds, but they should not be carried to the extent of separations.

Friendships, casual contacts, official contacts, business contacts, class or school mates, neighbors etc. fall into the category of separable. Of these can be close friends too. But this bond is need based and temporary. This can come to an end, once that need on which it is found is fulfilled or reaches to the point of saturation. As this point is reached, the casual talks, meets and exchange of greetings might still continue, but there won't be anything called bond, because with the saturation level, it's bonding life has expired.

Knowing that these are temporary and separable bonds, but still people give more priority, resources and time to them than to the inseparable. They treat the friends as brothers and sisters, but their siblings not even as friends. The amount of time they spend with friends is too big, the kind of relationship that they share with them is too close, the kind of emotions they share with them are full of laughter, entertainment, joyous and happy. The amount of resources they share with them are limitless and sacrificial. The same people when they go home into the inseparable bond, they are tight lipped, hardly spoken, serious, unloving, uncaring, selfish, mean, irresponsible and heartless too.

What a sad irony! The humans always live against the given laws, governing rules, functioning systems and right ways. They fail to understand the proper ways of living. The friends are not criticized here, neither is said that they shouldn't be sharing close bonds. The opposite is meant and expressed. Every bond should be stronger and unbroken. The orbital relationship comes into picture here. As every planet revolves in its designed orbit and fulfils it's given duties, so must also be the human relations. They must maintain their orbits of movement. Never should any of these ever try to cross over into another, which will result in disaster. The moment any planet tries to reduce the distance to the other, then there's always danger.

The first orbit is spousal. No one else should enter into this space. The second orbit is of offspring, they as siblings. Only parents and siblings are allowed into this orbit. The third is grandparents and relatives. They should be close and intact. The fourth one is friends and other need-based contacts, including neighbors. The parents must see that their kids spend quality time with them and with their siblings.

The bond of friendship must be maintained but they should neither jump from first orbit to the fourth nor the vice versa. Those kids who remain connected with their own, their first and their third orbit always, are rarely vulnerable to skip into any boy/girl relationships. They are also far from any kind of orbital dangers and disasters. Therefore, the mantra to safeguard your children from boy/girl and other disasters and dangers is 'keep them intact in their first, third and their own orbit.'

Mantra 24

MANY MOODS BUT ONE MODE

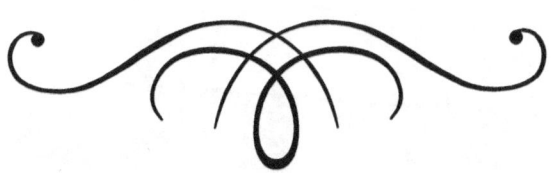

Lights and sounds, colors and textures, tastes and flavors, if exist only in one form, then life becomes monotonous. A variety of wide range is always the demand of every individual. The more the accessibility of many options and choices, the happier the heart of a man feels. With this happiness, man produces different tunes, rhythms and dances to match them. In this pursuit, man employs himself in constant discoveries and inventions. Billions of definitions and derivatives of the seen, heard, felt, and of the world are such products and byproducts.

With the emergence of so much in so many forms, the satisfaction or contentment meter in man's hearts disappeared. They are rarely seen in some in some matters, not in everything. Man of today has no understanding, that his satisfactory meter made its exit, way long back. Most people never ever realize that there is supposed to be anything called satisfaction, and they need to apply brakes reaching that point.

There is another world other than the seen and man lives in, and that is the one inside his own heart. There are produced so many thoughts and emotions. The implication results of these thoughts and emotions are categorized into good and bad reactions. There are no good or bad emotions, but only the outward or inward reaction of any thought or feeling. Of these reactions too, there are acceptable, tolerable, adjustable, bearable and excusable.

It also depends upon the kind of person against whom the emotions or reactions are projected. If they are something that are against the behavioral standards, but the person facing them is too mature, cool, calm and understanding in nature, then any reaction would be accepted. If the love of the receiving person exceeds and finds no limits to tolerate anything, then no reaction is a wrong or bad one. But for the rest of the world, every reaction matters, and there could be opposite action, equal or mightier. The most important part of parenting syllabus has to do with actions and reactions of emotions. The parents who succeed to create, manage and provide right emotions and best suitable reactions in their children are the most blessed, peaceful, joyful and happy. The reverse of this sees everyday hell with their children.

Parenting module must consider the primary or basic psychology creation, which comes along with thoughts, feelings and their reactions. Those with positive mindset, approach and dealings finds intellectual ways to release their reactions. They do also possess cool and calm nature. They work with brains but are never driven or dragged by emotions. They react in good sense, appealing and pleasant to all. They never allow the worries, cares, tensions, troubles, challenges, fears, failures, insults, criticisms etc. to reach their hearts for reaction. Since they work with brains, they know very well that such things must be stopped on the brain roads, and never allowed a gate pass to the heart roads. Such parents teach emotions creation and their management beautifully.

Raja and Rani, the exemplary parents of this learning have learnt and developed to manage the reactions to all the struggles, battles, conflicts, unpleasant happenings in themselves and between themselves. They learnt this art after so many misunderstandings, quarrels heartbreaks and losses. Both of them were very short tempered, swift to react and blunt to speak their hearts. They both actually regret after every harsh exchange, soon comes to compromise and leaving it for time to speak it out.

Eventually, this way of compromise, forgiving, forgetting, and deciding to live a quarrel free and fights free life enabled them to manage their emotions and their reactions. Since they have a dream and goal to create their sweet and happy heaven at home, and teach their children to be a part with same wave length, they focused to remove every wrong, bad and unacceptable reactions and throw them far away, where neither they themselves nor their children can ever go.

Stating the different reactions, that are mostly used by many to get their voice heard, opinions valued, things done and being accepted, the parents began teaching them that they are not acceptable and allowed at home. This training began when the kids were mere infants. If at all they need anything or happens anything to them, then crying, sobbing, lamenting, throwing tantrums, sitting silent in isolation, getting angry, protesting against food, locking inside, hurting self, destroying things etc. are not at all the acceptable, allowed or tolerable means.

They were strict in mentioning that, they may be coming across such ways of meeting their needs somewhere with friends, neighbors or everywhere in the world, but since theirs is a totally different and sweet world, such behaviors have no room in it. The world may be seeing it succeed through various unacceptable modes but their home must have only one mode, that is speaking openly, boldly and lovingly with the liberty they have provided.

Right from their infancy stages, Raja and Rani succeeded to teach their kids to ask for anything, report anything and complain anything, only in clear words, with no tears, no reactions. The kids didn't then develop any of the reactions of the world. They are not allowed any single moment to find themselves in isolation. They are always in the company of each other and of the parents. They are allowed to have a feeling of every emotion, spend little time in it, but when it comes to reaction and duration, only one mode and very little time. Kids, who are allowed to spend more time and repeatedly in wrong, bad, unacceptable behaviors to react, develop it as their tools to get things done, their nature and character.

The kids, Raj Kumar and Raj Kumari were given so much of freedom to enjoy their lives in every right and best possible manner. Their home is truly a heaven unto them. They long to return to it soon from anywhere and prefer more than any other place. There's lot of happiness and joy in them and in their home, because there are no wrong reactions for any emotion and happening. Therefore, the mantra for a heavenly home is, 'the world might have many moods, but a sweet home will have only one mode, speak out and rejoice.'

Mantra 25

CULPRIT HOME

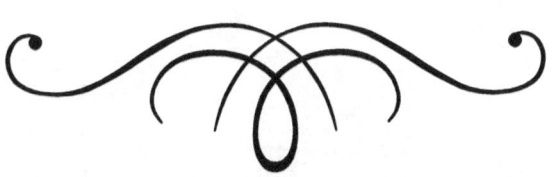

Human race is traced back to several thousand years before Christ Era and two thousand plus years post His era. It has seen so many changes and transformations in countless areas of what is there around it. It had passed through so many phases of love and hatred. The period of peace and harmony as a result of the sermons on love, and its projection among men across the globe was for a very short time. But the reign of hatred and violence still continues right from the very beginning of human history. Many messengers of love had taken the stage to spread its seeds and see the fruits, but all for little results or no results.

The God of love, stepped down into human space, as one among them, and resumed the role of the Messenger of Love, which many did before Him. Walking through the streets of Judea, Samaria and other neighboring regions, Jesus Christ constantly sowed the seeds of love, and also gave a command, 'love your neighbor as you love yourself.' The hatred world did not let the love, the messenger of love, also the God of love exist in its space for more time. He was brutally crucified by them that did not receive His message.

The world of today is still struggling to find answers to so many questions. It had been doing the same for ages and will continue to do so until it becomes extinct. If careful research is done to stop all these hurting and destroying happenings, the answer comes in just two words, and they are, indifference and inequality. As discussed in the previous lessons, the strife and battles between the spouses, among the siblings, relatives and friends are ghastlier than the World Wars. This is where the actual venom is produced in one form and later spread widely in another form. This indifference and inequality are the seeds that produce gender and racial enmities.

The feeling of being superior and the thirst for dominance demeans other gender and different complexion. The male gender feels that the world belongs to it and the female is an inferior and second grade citizen. The men thinks that all the privileges belong to them and the women survive at their mercy. The women world is denied of any right of the home, society and of the nation. She is still considered the weaker section of the society. And hence is restricted to the household chores.

Gender roles are thus defined by the dominant patriarchs and assigned to both of them. No role is defined or designed by the female gender; all those are done by the males. They have reserved all the public appearing, earning, fighting, ruling and force works to themselves. To the women they gave the household responsibilities, which includes cooking, scavenging, laundering and parenting. The men set themselves free from the women's works and from raising children. They feel the mother is responsible for bringing up children. Once the male child enters into teenage, then the father takes him out along only to teach the power works and authoritative responsibilities. But the girl child is left to remain with mother.

The blame for indifference and inequality sowing doesn't alone go onto the male gender, but also onto the female. She is not just equal partaker in this venomous seeding, but is to be blamed more than the male, because she always longs for a male child and treats him superior to female child, and transfers all privileges to him. Be it buying things, toys, vehicles, feeding food, choosing school and tuition, giving pocket money, excusing faults, allowing freedom, sending for picnics and tours etc. the mother leans unto her son or sons. Most parents don't want to spend on daughters, because one day she will become a part of another family. But the sons are worth investing in their sight, because they will bring returns tomorrow.

As learnt before, the home and the parents are the first place and people that the children are exposed and connected to, so all the learning takes place from them itself. All the good and all the bad comes initially from home. The impact of any learning, especially the bad from home becomes stronger. The child might be learning bad or wrong from somewhere else, but that impact cannot be more as long as the same is not practiced by the parents at home.

The parents can become good heroes and also bad heroes with bad character and conduct to their children. They might demonstrate bad, selfish, harsh, cruel, wicked, and devilish traits in front of their children and become their heroes, and encourage them to be the same. A thief might become a hero for his/her child with heroic way of robbery. A militant might get hero salute from his/her children for heroic ways of killing and escaping. A soft spoken, loving person might become hero to his/her children with the forgiving and surrendering act for taking the blame and settling the matter.

Parenting is not a skill or ability learnt, but a character developed worth exemplary. The two characteristics, indifference and inequality when removed from the hearts of parents, then the new generation will only develop love and harmony. The resultant will be, its spread everywhere. Parents must not differentiate the gender roles.

The boys and the girls must be taught all skills, abilities including the household chores equally. It should be taught from the very beginning, that they should be independent of doing their personal works and also consider it their responsibility to help parents. If any home appears to be the culprit for spreading hatred and enmity through indifference and inequality, then it should rethink today and decide whether to continue to produce venomous society or wants to become a contributor of spreading love and harmony for an equally privileged happy world. Therefore, the mantra for eradicating the indifference and inequality is 'catch hold of the culprit home and teach her love and harmony.'

Mantra 26

HOME THEATRE

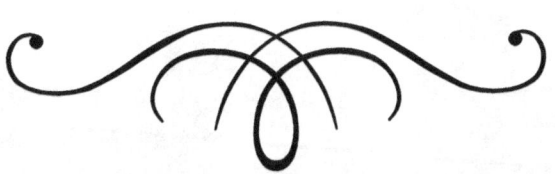

*D*ramatic were those early days, when scientific technology was making baby steps but was inventing and discovering many things. People with rich capacities were the only fortunate to own and experience them. The poor at finances had neither heard about them nor ever saw them until the television made its wide presence in the remote streets through the rich class. People began to peep inside the mansions to have a look at the Television screen and got to know the world far from them. Some generous hearts make them available to everyone by placing Televisions out in open space for communities to watch.

Telephone was one among such, that people began to see in use. That used to have three components, the device, the receiver and the mouth piece. Later it got developed into a single piece with both the receiver and the mouth piece. This has two people taking turns to speak and to listen. Sometimes, there appears only speakers at one end and only hearers at the other end. The speakers are brakeless ones and the hearers are full of patience and concern.

The world is a platform and everyone is a performer. The world platform is neither purposefully made nor do the performers on it consciously act. That is an ongoing day to day movement and the people are the moving characters, all doing various things only for their survival, for their learnings, for their extra earnings, for their entertainment and pleasures etc. There is a real stage purposefully made and consciously enacted; it requires watching eyes, hearing ears, clapping hands and praising mouths.

Boring and unsatisfactory would be the days of performances where the galleries pose pale look with empty stands. Not just these platforms, but every person carries a stage with him/her, wherever they go. All the people of the world have a story to tell, a song to sing, a dance to perform, something or the other all the time. And they need at least one person to hear and watch them. People then constantly engage themselves to search for audiences, spectators and readers. They make countless efforts to make them their permanent followers.

Coming from larger picture to the smaller one, an individual, who has something to say, need something to hear, that makes him/her feel good, accepted, loving, someone to accompany and someone to be with all the time. A lonely person feels singled out, rejected, unwanted, disliked, unpleasant as a result develops moody, depressed, irritated, angry, hateful, unfriendly, violent and destructive nature. Such people live in themselves and will be far from any heart to connect.

The other danger of being singled out is, such people will search for someone to connect themselves, and in that course, they will stop using any standards or principles for choosing friendship or making relationship. They just want someone, and will stick to the same upon finding even the opposite sex. That might end up in bad company or lead to a wrong relationship. Both are dangerous for the kids at growing stages, and incurable pain and heartache to parents. This would be a dead end; it closes all the doors for escape. Not many finds the will and way to escape from it. Fortunate, blessed, strong willed, wise and open eyed are those that makes early U turn and focuses on studies and good morals.

Kids at home must find it their stage/platform and their parents and siblings their first eyes, ears, hands and mouths to watch, hear, clap and praise. This is not just for any of their talents performed, but for everything they want to say, show and do. If the closed knit family, the parents and the siblings become their home theatre, then the kids will never look for any outsider to confide in. They won't need any others company and love when too much of it is found at home. Always listen to them, even that is very silly. Look at them, even when you are busy in work. Appreciate them, even if they are not up to the mark. Praise them for all their efforts and attempts.

When parents distance them and make their relationship point to point business, then kids would limit themselves before them for point to point appearances. This would result in broken relations and broken families. Therefore, the mantra to keep your kids not long for bad and wrong company, not to see theirs and your lives ruined is, 'become their home theatre, let that be always on. Be available for them. Be with them. Let them feel comfortable and secure in your loving presence.'

Mantra 27

NO MOOD DAY

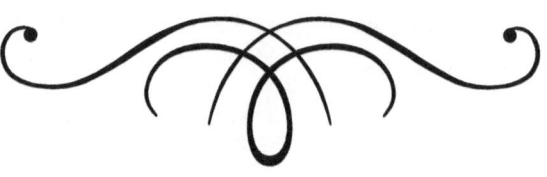

Who can stop the negative, who has the capacity to restrict the bad, who will save himself from being influenced, who can forever stand without falling, who can keep succeeding without failing, who can say 'I am without imperfections, I am perfectly perfect?' Not even a single person would dare to make these claims false on him. As the earth has the pulling force against the opposite of it, so is the man prone to fall, and must keep himself to work constantly to stand against those pulling and pushing forces. It is not an occasional or just a day-to-day process, but a time to time one.

No one is without fall, no one is without weaknesses, no one is without temptations, no one is without curiosity to at least make one attempt and experiment the forbidden or the prohibited. The forbidden and the prohibited are the ones possessing bad, wrong, harmful and dangerous character. The one who is aware of their bad effects categorized them to unapproachable and untouchable list, and will warn others too to stay away from them.

Instructions regarding careful living often fall into deaf ears. Wrong practices and bad behavior will make their way to the very careful and the careful by some way or the other. Especially the growing kids are vulnerable to them, may be due to curiosity or 'experiment and experience mindset'. Some can be allowed once or twice, but if not monitored and put a check, it can lead to harmful and dangerous practices.

Skipping school and other classes, not feel like studying, having playful mood, be awake till late night, rise up late too, skipping meals, skipping shower and brushing teeth, be disorganized, allow laziness are some among such. For that, they will make excuses of not keeping well. In cases of little temperature, cold, cough, though can go and submit assignments, projects, give exams, but still the mind says to skip them. Some kids make this regular practice, their parents do not bother to rectify this, rather they back their children with wrong support. Such children rarely attend the classes. They find a silly reason, like the visitation of some relatives, attending a wedding, festival, religious practices etc.

Raj Kumar and Raj Kumari are no exceptions. They too have all the weaknesses and temptations like other kids. Though, they are perfectly raised under careful parenting, but still they possess that vulnerability of being tempted, influenced and impacted. They watch others and question themselves, 'when something is not wrong or bad to some parents, why that is to our parents? Why other parents allow their kids miss the school, classes and internal exams too, but our parents don't?' Sometimes, they do let these signals get released out of their brains and hearts, but they have signal receiving parents, who can catch and read them well.

The parent couple understands them and allows them to meet their harmless prohibited experiences. Sometimes, they would see that the kids are not that active and giving them a break would refresh them and heal completely, they would give an option, if they don't feel like going to school, then it is okay with them. If they wish to go, that is also okay. The kids would make the first choice. This kind of choices comes only once or twice in an academic year. They don't allow this to become their habit and regular practice.

Sometimes, they don't feel like studying, then the parents allow them to play for some time, listen to music, take out their bicycles and go riding, or do something that would refresh their minds. After the allowed 'no mood time or a no mood day,' the kids must seriously concentrate in their prime duty, study. Weekends and holidays are their rightful free days from all academic learning, but they would be engaged into some vacation camps. Therefore, the mantra for a relaxed and refreshed mind, that can be more active and sharper than ever before is, 'allow no mood times and no mood days as and when they are very necessary.'

Mantra 28

END OF PREACHING AND PUNISHING

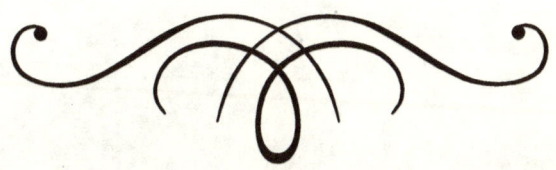

The set up is the primary structure and the basic foundation of any construction. Having an idea in mind for a small, medium, large and huge sized design for any purpose, the first and foremost before laying its foundation is having the set up taken out of mind and brought into reality. The rest is addition to make it complete. An application file in the computer comes as a set up. The rest are add-ons and updates. The add-on files don't have installation and working nature unless they are brought into the structure of the set-up application. They cannot work on their own. Once the setup is done, all other advancements come as updates and keep renewing the older versions.

The billboards on the roadside are the face of a huge metal structure supported with strong pillars, deeply fixed in the ground. A circus cannot take place just because they have artists, animals and adventurers. It takes the shape of a circus only after the primary set up is installed. A movie studio consists of several setups catering to various scenic needs. Hundreds of movies are made in the same studio, using the basic structures, by changing colors, designs, positions, internal and external shapes and items.

There's no limit for any advanced and research learning if the foundational education is properly laid in man. The basics at school grades can further shape him into an educationist, scientist, agriculturist, artist, architect, doctor, engineer, designer etc. The high school learning is the basic set up of education system, the higher secondary grades are initial add-ons to choose the path that would lead to future profession and career.

Many other learnings that include skills and technology are additional add-ons that would strengthen and add more caliber to the actual frame of mainstream learning. Awareness, support and encouragement unto such can bring out a multi skilled, multi abilities personality with excellence. Identifying the inborn qualities that would express themselves in the form of dream, passion, desire, interest; observing the learning capacities, man must be provided access and provision for digging them out.

Proportions and measures, limits and boundaries tell that anything beyond this will spoil, trespass and attract unpleasant reaction. Too much of anything loses its appealing and pleasing quality. Repeat of that too much is either unaccepted or is sent into thrash. Too many gifts surely bring lots of joy and excitement, but being too many, they have already lost their long life. One or few gifts that would draw the attention and make them used will be of more value than so many dividing the attention and interest, such would attract no heart and value. Too much of wealth, either increases the greed for more or spoils the heart for prodigal living. Too little resources are always helpless and useless tools; too many, unorganized and scattered are pointless and time spoilers.

Parenting involves canes and sword like tongues, it has blazing bloody eyes and fierce face. A concerned and cautious parent never spares the cane, a loving and caring parent doesn't allow the heart to overtake mind and brain. A wise parent believes the structural set up and is fully focused to bring it into his/her child. He/

she knows that installing the application set up called discipline is the success of a well-mannered and career focused individual. Since this set up is the basic and foundational, it should be laid in stages of infancy to adolescence. All the strictness, usage of canes, fiery-red bloody eyes, fierce faces and swordy tongues must end at pre-teen stages. At teens, the add-ons of preaching and demonstrating must add more colors and flavors to the basic structures.

Those who believe in laying foundational structures at teenage have already lost the grip over their children. Parents who continue to extend this structural set up post teens will attract rebellion and back answers. Knowing the disciplining methods, timings, stages and means will help bringing out a glorious child, and they in return will produce blessed parents. The preaching must be stopped when the demonstration contradicts the former. Preach as long as the same is projected, unless it will attract disrespect and displeasure. Therefore, the mantra to see a perfectly raised offspring is, 'know when to preach and when to punish.'

Mantra 29

MAKE AMBITIOUS

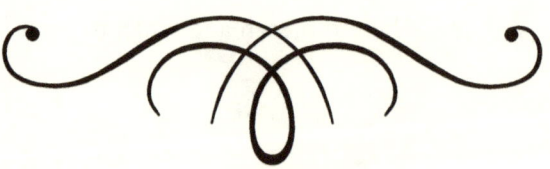

Advancing in age is said to be the sign and evidence of maturity and wisdom. It is also known as the stage of having learnt and mastered various subjects and areas of life. It usually walks parallel with perfection. It uses more of understanding than any other emotions and feelings. It finds itself acquired huge quantity of love and compassion, and that they should be shared with and poured upon everyone. It cannot tolerate any injustice and inhuman nature.

Maturity lets go off silly, petty and harmless mistakes with a beautiful smile on face. It ignores many issues, and if need arises, handles well without using any strong emotions. Many are the best and positive sides of reaching mature stage, advancing in age and experiences. Some at this point loses control over many life systems. For them, passing the time in any way stands their only business of life. This can be seen in them who are retired from service and other vocations.

Having grandparents, relatives along with many offspring all around is the real matter that brings exceeding joy to family oriented and purpose focused person. Kids will be favored with great company and enjoyment in such closed knit family. Finding privacy in such setups proves to be the greatest challenge. A personal study space and suitable time may be equal to winning medals and trophies. Thousands of generations have passed through this stage and proved themselves champions, excelling in several areas of life. Nothing hindered them to do what they wanted to.

The beauty of relationships and living in harmony is a great favor by such family setups. The world had narrowed itself to nuclear living, with just very few members in the family. But still, the parenting stands out as a greatest challenge before the majority of the world. Making their kids sit for studies and bringing them up in good atmosphere, even though with all provisions, privacy, personal study space and facilities becomes a daily hard task.

When the parents realize that they are the initial eyes, ears, minds and other senses of their children, then they would be seeing, hearing, feeling and thinking first, on behalf of them. As the caring parents take all the harsh and hurting things like direct sunlight, cold weather and rains over themselves and protect their new born and infants, so must they take all the responsibility of their future too. Not everyone in the family is strongly determined, perfectly focused, well organized and career oriented. If the father is so, then the mother may not be.

It can be true in the reverse of it. Sometimes, either of them seems to be unfocused or vice versa. If the focused is making the child study more and enrolling in various vocations, task mastering, then the other spouse or grandparents, or some relative might see that as harsh and hurting burden. All their love, compassion and other caring emotions squeezes their hearts and hinder the training parent. The children, if least bothered about daily works and assignments, would find the people around them as saviors, who helps them get rid of more hours of learning and additional vocations.

The primary duty of the parents then involves in making their children see their future in the beginning itself. No doubt, almost all the parents make their children speak out what they wanted them to become in the future. But that remains only for that infancy stage where they make the babies speak out in playful mode. That vanishes from their focus as the children gets enrolled in the school and distances themselves for greater time of the day.

Ideal parents must let this goal, aim and ambition installed in their kids and make constant reminders to keep it alive. The kids that have this installation done in them, makes a habit to undergo extra assignments and vocations. They won't care to the sympathizing words of others, grandparents and relatives. They see them as necessary advancements for ambitious present and achieved future.

Teaching their kids to think, reason out and resist the enemy, that distracts them from primary focus, including the sympathy of the loving and caring ones, without letting them losing qualitative moments of life, should be another greater task of artful parenting. Functions in the family, social gatherings, festivals etc. should not consume more than the limited and allowed time of learning and growing kids. Training them to fix their all senses on the aimed goal and rest not until they reach there, makes them ambitious, thinking big, aiming big and attempting bigger things. Therefore, the mantra for seeing future in the present is, 'setting milestones as shorter goals and the finish lines as the ultimate goals. To achieve that, making their nature completely focused with ambitious attitude installed in them is the only way.'

Mantra 30

STOP COMPARING AND TAUNTING

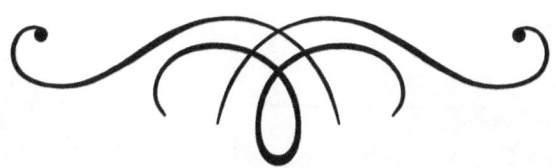

Any offender, accused of offence or a suspect of offence gets a file opened on their name at the local police station. The police then first asks them to reveal everything and accept if at all, the accusation is true. Anything of not that serious concern, which doesn't attract much punishment, is either brought to a compromise between the accuser and the accused, or if proven, the accused is released with few hours of lockup punishment. But if the offence is big and is not proved, then the offender is produced in the court.

All the evidences and witnesses are attached to prove him/her guilty. All these make way to stand before the judge and plead either guilty or innocent. This is the first and the last time the charged faces the judge. The judge after hearing all the final arguments, witnesses and the charged, writes the sentence either guilty or innocent. After pronouncing what was written, the judge then disappears from the sight of entire investigating teams and the accusers and the accused. There won't be any other instance of meeting the judge, unless and until there is another offence against the same.

The judge upon the same offender will mostly ask him as to why he repeats such acts. But that won't affect in his hearing to the present case. Judge will only recollect the accused and the previous judgement. He won't allow his mind to preoccupy those thoughts and affect on the ongoing judgement process. Judging procedure has no place for emotions or feelings. That consists only facts, evidences, witnesses, arguments and the law. Even if it happens that the repeat offender might be facing the same judge several times, but that doesn't grant him to pronounce harsh punishment. The law only works on the quantum of punishment for each case. It doesn't repeat the punishment for already closed file and undergone period.

Parents, while dealing punishable behavior of the children, usually recollects all the past acts too and allow their anger take mad form and punish them very badly. Many a times, parents taunt their children repeatedly and connect everything to the past behavior, failures, mistakes or damages. When children do not fare well in their respective duties, parents consider them unworthy of any privileges. They even restrict them from buying favorites, having delicacies, outing, entertainment and play times.

Since the children are not up to the mark, and are the reason for parent's shame in their circles and also to make them mad, they feel cutting down or restricting them of their privileges will put them back in track. Different parents apply different measures, methods and ways to correct their children. It's okay. But the repeat of the punishment for something new, taunting all the time and cutting down or restricting privileges or rights is not the proper way. Give them the best, speak to them and make them understand in the best way. Do not be harsh and cruel while punishing.

Some parents have the tendency to compare with others all the time. They never seem to be satisfied with what their children do or achieve. Be it the conduct or discipline, academics or achievements, they see somebody else better than their children.

They express a heart to appreciate them and accept their everything as up to the mark, but they are never satisfied with their own children. This comparison disheartens their children and cause to lose respect unto themselves first. They do start to disrespect their parents as well. They might feel to drop themselves from any further betterment or attempt to do anything. This also reduces their enthusiasm for becoming anything in life and zeal to live.

Comparisons and taunts are no tools for expecting betterment and disciplined behavior. They are negative weapons which destroys all good qualities to keep going. Strict parenting is good, but if accompanied by equal amount of love and understanding, then it is the best. There's nothing that love and care cannot win, change or subdue. There's nothing that cannot be solved with talk of understanding. Even the wars and the world wars end or doesn't take place at all with cordial talks.

Parents of understanding apply cool minds and loving hearts while dealing with children's issues. They bring in wisdom and knowledge to teach, correct and discipline. Parents desiring to see greater achievements, excellent performances and wonderful beings in their children will never demean, disrespect, discredit, degrade them, but allow them a dignified life. Therefore, the mantra to transform the worst of the performances or see better conduct in your children is, 'stop comparing, taunting and start appreciating for the performed, achieved and encourage for better and the best.' A heart to forgive, overlook, ignore the grave misconduct and utter poor performances, and applying cool mind and loving heart with correcting talk can pull up from the valleys and push onto the highest mountain peaks.

Mantra 31

COMPLAINING MOMS AND BASHING DADS

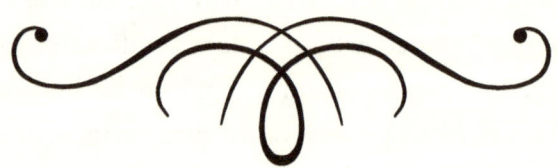

Rainfall is no person's friend other than the farmers and the residents of parched lands. It is no man's joy other than children, who love to play in it all the day and get drenched. Nonstop constant rains hinder many works; when turned into flood and storm, destroys greater extent. Upon crossing the limit of absorption of the land and finding no way for the flow into harmless locations, the land and all that on it will lose their shape and value.

Many suffer so badly that their senses don't work to find a way out. They cannot stop the rains, they cannot stop it flooding, they cannot change the nature of the land for long time even after the rains stopped. Unless the sunlight favors on it, nothing can turn it into fertile and useful again. It cannot be denied that it is the rain alone that makes the harvested land reusable, but not without the sunlight, and with excess of rains.

Canes and rulers are the straighteners in child's growing ages. They are the tools to produce fear and responsibility. They are their benefactors and future makers. They are inevitable pain givers as long as they don't mend ways for picking up the straight path. They do rain on them sometimes, depending upon the severity of the matter or the extent of parent's anger. Children cannot resist them, they cannot stop them, they cannot avoid them, they cannot escape them, they cannot do anything other than facing them. Just like the constant monsoon rains are unstoppable, so are the raining canes and rulers of the angry parents.

Sensible parents use them sparingly and only when needed. Moody parents consider them their stress busters and mood setters. Angry parents see them as the only means and modes to compensate for the poor performance and bad conduct. Stubborn and foolish parents never separate them from themselves even upon the child grown into a young adult. Teachers at school, tutors at tuition centers feel that they are cent percent marks scorers. Maximum people love to pick them up in their hands upon seeing the little children. Some cruel natured finds them as the means of entertainment, when they are rained upon the little ones, when they cry out and roll down in pain. Inhuman and beastly natured sees them as pleasure tools to torture and get wicked happiness.

Little children suffer many beatings, tortures, abuses and violence from the parents, grownup siblings, relatives, neighbors, teachers, tutors and even from strangers too. They have no power to resist, they have no courage to stop, they are not equipped to escape the predators, they are not so matured to understand what's happening on them. Many are the powerful negative effects that hit such children, and they play the destroyer role all through their upbringing.

People of cowardice, slow mind, dumb nature, traumatized heart, introvert behavior and poor grades are one such possibility downwards the normal line. People of arrogance, disrespect, hatred, violent, abusive, cruel, beastly, stubborn, inattentive, scaring and terrifying behavior is the other side of the normal line, moving harshly upwards, but with negative and bad life.

Some children are blessed with parents of love, care, concern, understanding, encouraging, motivating, providing, helping, guiding, protecting and friendly nature. Some are blessed with few of the foresaid, but doesn't find bad or poor parenting. Some are hit with very bad and worst parenting. Parenting as repeatedly mentioned here suggests proper awareness of the dos and do nots, complaining moms and bashing dads are a strict no for any parent.

Moms usually find themselves powerless before their children, because they don't listen to them and care for their word. Such moms take the help of dads. They produce the fear of father's strictness and warn their children to report any matter they won't heed to. In this course, they complain to their husbands against their children. Gradually, moms become complainers and dads becomes bashers. This nature leads to constant complaints and regular bashings.

No child ever likes either of them. Every child needs the parents as loving and friendly natured, who can keep them from any harsh treatments of every other; those who can bring them up delicately and handling with lots of care. If the children are brought up in hurting ways, then only useless and dummies are produced. Exceptional are those that are life focused and rise against every worst happening and makes their career. But the sweet and lovely childhood turned bitter and painful. Who can reverse them, who can heal them and who can better them? Therefore, the mantra to gift your children sweet memorable childhood is, 'do not become a complaining mom and bashing dad.'

Mantra 32

ARE YOU SATISFIED

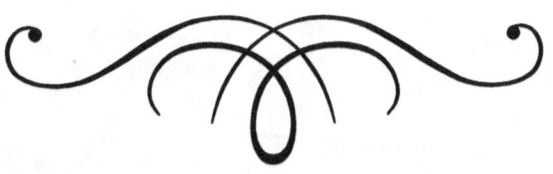

A golfer after hitting the long shot walks all the way to find where it landed. Usually, it won't be traveling straight to the targeted area. Since that is very far and the hole or cup is not visible clearly. Sometimes, the ground consists of hills and slopes. The golfer can see the erected flagpole indicating the hole and based on it makes his target shot. There is a possibility that the ball reaches somewhere the pointed target, but not inside the cup or hole. The opponent also makes his first shot. The golfer, his opponent, the referee and the equipment carriers known as a caddie walks along to the spot where the ball landed. The area is marked with ball markers and the golfers take turns to repeat shots. The second shot is a mere slow push that aimed to pocket the ball. Celebrations follow upon pocketing the ball, the golfer is appreciated for his efforts to qualify himself and to excel in his deliveries.

Parenting is something similar to such sports, where every sportsperson checks and rechecks until the deliveries are landed at the targeted spots and made best use of them. A periodic check consisting an honest talk with lots of questions and so much of listening would reveal whether the deliveries in parenting are actually needed to the children, are they receiving them, are they helpful tools or hurting weapons, do they like their parents or feel they should be like others. A task mastery type of parenting involves just giving instructions, directions and commands with targets to accomplish. A true parenting involves knowing the heart of children and knowing honestly what do they feel about them. If needed, should be humble and frank enough to correct themselves.

Raja and Rani would sit together with their children and talk for hours periodically. They would be putting several questions before them, one after the other and wait to hear them out. After the kids respond, they then would be drawing parallels and comparing the kind of life they got, facilities, provisions, standards of living, kind of parenting etc. They would speak and let the children understand the different kinds of parenting and upbringings. In matters of finances and wealth, their friends' parents may be well ahead and ultra rich, but in matters of other things like the kind of happiness and joy of living, they see themselves more blessed than anyone.

Parents make them know that each person has their own taste, style and focus of life. No one matches the other exactly. Some could be limiting themselves to necessary mode of living, some for more comforting, some for luxurious and extravagance. Some might be walking on foot to school, some use public transport, some go by two wheelers, some use four wheelers. Some would be living on rented small houses, some owned small house, some in apartments and some having big bungalows and farm houses. It doesn't matter who owns what and lives for what. What matters is, is everyone living right and happy?

Since this family is a believer of Jesus Christ, hopes and waits for eternal life in heaven, and the entry into it is prohibited for a sinner with sinful living, and the commandments of the Bible demands a pure character, free from all substances of tobacco, alcohol and drugs, forbidden from speaking bad and behaving wrong, they have laid the basic foundations on them. That is the reason these parents teach their children the affects and effects of wrong living.

They tell their children that, some of your friend's parents might not have any problem if they get into school bunking, exam skipping, indisciplined behavior, fighting, quarrels, abusive words, vulgar language, smoking, drinking, having boy girl relationships, rude and disobedient to teachers; problematic to neighbors and everyone; scoring poor marks, failing grades, watching television, surfing internet, playing games all the time etc. But your parents have a problem if you tend to live this way.

The children Raj Kumar and Raj Kumari adopted this lifestyle and felt it more comfortable and happier than any other, since they found themselves free from all unnecessary troubles, distracting social life, degrading corrupt behavior, disrespectful image, greedy nature, competitive longing, complaining attitude, provocative temperament, lustful temptations etc. They found a good friend in their parents, who are understanding enough with lots of care, full of wisdom and knowledge, encouraging and motivating. They have someone who had dedicated themselves completely for caring and loving parenting. The most beautiful part is to listen and know from their kids about their deliveries and frank and humble enough to accept and change the wrongs, whether intentional or unintentional. Therefore, the mantra to hit the target is, 'walk along, sit together and spend quality time; be frank and humble to learning. Ask your children, whether they are satisfied and happy with you.'

Mantra 33

MAKE YOUR OWN

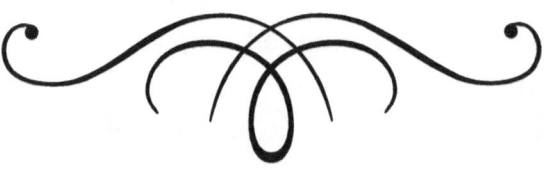

A teacher at certain institute after every life session would give them a seed each to all his students and asks them to plant them and have a beautiful garden. The month-long course with various lessons, ideas, thoughts and exercises accompanied thirty different seeds. The teacher told his students that his last session, the most important one would be after a month. He would also wish to see their beautiful garden then.

The students were not so serious about the seeds and the garden. They just prepared themselves to appear for the examination. On that scheduled day of last session all the students and the teacher got together for the final session. He gave them the last lesson on sincerity, honestly, truthfulness, duty and accountability. At the end, he said there will be test on all the learnings of the month. But for that he needs to see the oldest and the youngest plant from each one's gardens. They ought to carry them to the class next day and appear for the exam.

The following day all the students made their presence with two plants each in their hands. One was tall and the other was shorter than that. All the students brought in same kind of plants and also of same size. The teacher upon examining all their plants appreciated them very well. He asked them how many plants altogether they have. Their response was thirty. Teacher asked them again, had everyone managed to keep all the plants alive. Yes, came the answer from all of them. But there was a student, an odd man out from the entire class.

He came empty handed, but was more confident and bolder than the rest who carried their plants. The teacher enquired that lone student to explain the reason for his empty hands and sat in front of him patiently and waited for his answer. He told the teacher that his hands were empty because of honesty and truthfulness. He said, they were also empty because of sincerity. Actually, he did not feel it was his duty to sow seeds. He did not go there to make a garden, rather simply follow the instructions for life lessons. He never thought that there would be accountability too. But the last lesson prior to this was final reason for his empty hands.

Before that student could explain anything more in detail, he asked the rest to explain, how did they manage to get the same size and same kind of plants. Each one almost varied in their explanation. The teacher said, 'you all have lied beautifully, none of you were sincere, honest, truthful, duty bound and accountable. But I wish to hear the lone student, why all the aforesaid are the reasons for his empty hands and why was he not expecting accountability.

He said, he did not sow any of the seeds at first. Second, he changed his mind not to buy the ready grown from the nursery. Third, he doesn't know what kind of seeds they were. Fourth, he felt to accept his faults sincerely and correct himself to be accountable for himself first and following every lesson next his duty. The teacher then turned to the entire class and said, this was the test and you all have failed. He had given everyone different seeds, moreover the dead seeds which can never sprout. You all have purchased the plants from nurseries. The lone pass out is none other than the lone odd man out. The teacher finally said, 'every teaching and learning is only for you. If you follow and apply them in life, then they will give life to you.'

Raja and Rani having given this example to their children made their final teaching and preaching. They said, 'from here on you will only be reminded, corrected and rectified. The foundations are laid in you, now it is your turn to erect a suitable, long lasting, beautiful and lovely building upon them.' They said that the parenting never ends at any stage of life, but takes another mode of overseeing, guiding and leading from behind.

The parents also told their children that, they may not be satisfied with many things in life, they may be having several suggestions and ideas to parent them, many insufficiencies, forceful adjustments and compelling compromises, but that is the best being their parents they could provide. 'Few years from now, you will be making your own families, have these in your hearts as motivators and driving forces to gift your children the best, but don't allow them as bitter feelings and hurting unmet desires. Failing to do so, you will never get the satisfaction of the sweet best you have in life.'

Having reached the last Mantra of 33 Marvelous Mantras For Artful Parenting, all through the course, many methods, methodologies, secrets, mantras, advices, techniques and models have been presented. They are apt and sufficient to have a control over your children and you become their best and exemplary parents. The careful following of all these mantras would create a beautiful and loving family with all the blessedness of life.

This will also produce joy and happiness along with unbreakable bond of harmony and unity. The kids will not just respect their parents, fear them, obey, follow, but will also love them wholeheartedly, long to be with them than anyone else, make their ways for excellence in every respect of life and become the source of peace and heavenly atmosphere. The last mantra of Artful Parenting is 'remember all the 32 mantras, follow them diligently and sincerely. Your honesty and truthfulness to learn and implement in life would produce sweet home and sweethearts.'

www.ingramcontent.com/pod-product-compliance
Lightning Source LLC
LaVergne TN
LVHW041710070526
838199LV00045B/1289